# GOING TO

CW00481059

*A BIKE RIDE A(*

By

*STEVE CUTHBERTSON*

blog.goingtothedogs.co.uk

# INTRODUCTION

There's a book in everyone, so they say… Well, let's see if there's a book in me, shall we?

Actually, this would be the third book I've started, but I've failed to finish the other two, so hopefully I can do a little better on this occasion.

This is a follow-on effort to my bike rides in support of Amicii Dog Rescue UK – who rescue dogs from the UK and overseas. Their kennels are in Worcester from where they re-home many dogs. They have re-homed over 2500 in the UK and many dogs from other countries.

All proceeds from the sale of this book will go to Amicii wherever possible – see legal notes.

I hope you enjoy reading it!

# TABLE OF CONTENTS

# Legal Notes

All the information in this book is published in good faith and for general information purposes only. I do not make any warranties about the completeness, reliability and accuracy of this information. Any action you take upon the information you find on this book, is strictly at your own risk. I will not be liable for any losses and/or damages in connection with the use of this book.

I will endeavour to donate all profits from this book to Amicii Dog Rescue UK on a periodic basis. Note: any profits will not automatically be donated, as this would require Amicii to set up a Kindle Direct Publishing account themselves, with their banking details, which I do not have access to. Instead, should there be any profits from this book, I will manually transfer such value to Amicii on a periodic basis.

# Chapter 1. Stella

I'm not quite sure when it occurred to me to fund-raise for Amicii by riding my bike. All I can tell you is that back in February 2023 I was acquiring the Amicii logo so I could get it printed on a cycling shirt, so it must have been in the depths of winter. Prior to April 2021 I don't think I'd even heard of Amicii, but that was all to change.

We already had two dogs, so I'm not sure why I was surfing the web looking for another, but there she was, the cutest looking, scruffy girl I'd ever seen. OK, so I'm biased.

Stella was found abandoned and close to death in a forest near Moldovenești, Romania. In the words of Cristina, the veterinary student (lucky for Stella) that found her, "we found her abandoned at the edge of a forest, she was sitting there on a sack and she was very, very thin".

After nurturing her back to health, Worcester-based charity Amicii brought her back to the UK and put her up for adoption. Unfortunately, poor Stella had some false starts. She went out to foster with a couple of different people, but sadly she proved too much for them and she ended up back at the rescue again after only a few days.

My wife Jill and I contacted Amicii and arranged to visit the kennels for a "meet and greet" – just an initial short meeting to see if we could get on with each other. We both sat in the courtyard nervously while Stella was brought out to meet us. I took a back seat on this occasion, as Stella had been described as "nervous around men". Thinking back to that meeting now, I remember Stella coming out and running around the courtyard – acknowledging our presence, but nothing more than that. Not friendly, not unfriendly. Still cute though. I'm still biased.

A couple of days later we were back – this time with our Cocker Spaniel, Dizzy and Alaskan Malamute, Iris, who despite the name, was a boy, (actually, he was a Huskamute, but that's another story) in tow – for an extended "meet and greet" in a nearby field. If they got on, or at least if they didn't take an instant dislike to each other, that would be the decision made.

In the field, things went OK. The spaniel ran around in circles in a manner that only spaniels can and the Huskamute didn't take much notice of Stella. There was a little interaction between them; not a lot, but enough to set our minds at rest. It was a done deal.

On the way home, Dizzy and Iris went in the boot (of the estate car) and Stella went on the back seat with Jill. She had a harness and seat belt on, but that

didn't stop her from deciding to sit on Jill's lap and try and stick her head out of the window.

At home, we gave Stella her own space in the kitchen and kept the other two dogs away with stair gates, so she had some space to call her own. We'd been briefed on the 3x3x3 rule which, in simple terms, says that it takes 3 days for your new dog to decompress from travel, 3 weeks for them to learn your routine, and 3 months for them to truly feel at home.

We didn't try to rush things in the slightest. Stella fell in to the dog-walking routine very easily. I'm an early riser, so dog walks at 5am were order of the day, usually about 3 to 4 miles. It soon became obvious however, that Stella was "reactive". Reactive to just about everything. People, dogs, cars, lorries, cats — you name it, she lunged at it. Fortunately, at 5am there aren't so many people, dogs, cars, lorries and even cats about, but even so, Stella was often found flying at the end of the lead. Gradually, with positive reinforcement (and bribery with biscuits) these tendencies became less and less. She still took her time to settle in though. Gradually she decided that the living room might be "safe", although on many occasions she took a step in to the room, then turned around and ran back to her bed in the kitchen.

Eventually, she made herself at home and was happy to come in to the living room in the evening and settle down next to us. Nowadays she's right at home. So

much so that she's quite happy to tell us when it's bedtime and that we should turn off the box with pictures and go upstairs. Should we ignore her, she just stomps off upstairs in a huff and goes to bed on her own!

So that's Stella, the still slightly-edgy, independent Romanian Shepherd (although a DNA test found just about everything in the mix) that follows me around like a shadow.

Stella is the reason behind the rest of the pages in this book.

# Chapter 2. Cycling

I've always been a fairly keen cyclist. Ever since I started secondary school at 11 years old, cycling had been my preferred mode of transport. I'd cycle the couple of miles to school and back every day, come rain or shine. I still remember my first "proper" bicycle - it was a turquoise three-speed bike of dubious manufacture. It wasn't new, of course, I didn't get my first new bike until I saved up my pocket money and bought it myself. Dad had picked it up somewhere and stripped it and painted it up for me. My sister also had a turquoise bike too. Must have had a job-lot of paint! Of course what I really wanted was a bike with drop handlebars - a "racer", as we used to call them. I'm not sure when the conversion of my flat bars happened, or where the set of "drops" came from, but I got my wish. The bike still only had three gears, with the ubiquitous Sturmey-Archer hub gear. I don't think it was in the best of health, to be honest, as sometimes I could only find two speeds in it and sometimes (usually when I was out of the saddle climbing a hill) second gear used to slip, leaving my legs spinning, or worse, skinning my shins with the metal "rat trap" pedals.

A key moment in my pursuit of cycling was to occur when the local cycling club was to stage a "criterium" through the streets of Taunton. A "crit" is a short circuit race on closed roads consisting of multiple laps. There are prizes, of course for the first over the line at the finish, but the race is kept more interesting by races within the race. Every couple of laps, there might be a "prime" (pronounced "preem"), which could gain the race leader at that time a cash prize. There may also be points for intermediate sprints during the race, with a separate prize for the leader on points at the end of the race. The result is a fast-paced competition, with constant attacks, counter attacks, thrills and spills. As an impressionable teen the experience was obviously memorable. During the race the announcer commented that for those who had enjoyed the spectacle and were interested in perhaps experiencing a little more participation, the local club had arranged a "beginners" club run the following weekend. I needed no further encouragement and from then on, I was hooked.

Fast-forward 40 years though and although I was still a keen cyclist, I seemed to have developed a distinct middle-aged spread. The form of a racing snake had long-since deserted me and I was very much a "fat man on a bicycle". I used to commute regularly from Kidderminster to Worcester by bike though and this must have given me some kind of "baseline" fitness – enough for me to ride from Land's End to John O'Groats (LEJOG) in 2014 in aid of Cancer Research UK.

Up until this year, LEJOG was my most ambitious foray in to long-distance cycling...

*John O'Groats, 2014*

# Chapter 3. A Plan

A man, a plan, a canal, Panama. A palindrome is a word, sentence, verse, or even number that reads the same backward or forward. Oh dear, Steve's gone off on a tangent. I can't say "a plan" without recounting a tale from 1996, when I was sitting next to Sir Ranulph Fiennes's hospital bed in Chile. For some obscure reason we ended up discussing palindromes. That was his. My best effort was "rotorvator". That's probably why he was described by the Guinness Book of Records as the world's greatest living explorer and I am not. Anyway, that's another story. Perhaps I should write a book?

As previously stated, I'm not sure when the idea occurred, but by February 2023 I was gradually building up the miles, cycling further and further each weekend. I'm still wasn't entirely sure what the plan was, apart from that it involved cycling long distances! To this end, I started undertaking "Audax" rides. Audax is a cycling sport in which participants attempt to cycle long distances within a pre-defined time limit. It's not a race. success in an event is measured by its completion. I completed a 200km ride and a 300km ride in March, another 300km ride and a 400km ride in April. Then I failed miserably at a 600km ride in May due to saddle-sores. Saddle-sores have always been a problem for me. In my 2014 LEJOG I rode hundreds of miles with a worsening sore, that eventually developed in to an open wound about the size of a fifty pence coin. I only completed LEJOG with a copious amount of anaesthetic cream and two pairs of shorts.

This is how I found myself explaining to Ann at Amicii only a couple of weeks after my failed 600km Audax:

*Me: Hi, I'm planning on doing a bike ride, fundraising for Amicii, what is the best way?*

*Ann: Sorry didn't mean to call - dog stood on phone*

*Me: OK. I am planning on cycling from Worcester kennels to Immingham kennels. In a day.*

*Ann: Omg! That's a b****y long way*

*When? Do you need anything? A place to stay when you arrive for example?*

*A lift?!!*

*Me: Should be OK. I will drive to Worcester and leave my car there and Jill can collect me from there. No idea how long it will take, but I'm guessing 13 or 14 hours minimum.*

*Ann: Wow. When are you planning this madness?*

*Me: Not 100% sure. I've been training though. Maybe 3rd June*

*Ann: Oh blimey OK x that's very soon!! Do you need anything? Logos/cycling tops??*

*Me: No, should be OK.*

*Ann: Great we will help to promote it, it's a lovely thing to do thank you so much x*

The die was cast, as the saying goes. I'd committed myself. Or I should have been committed. One or the other.

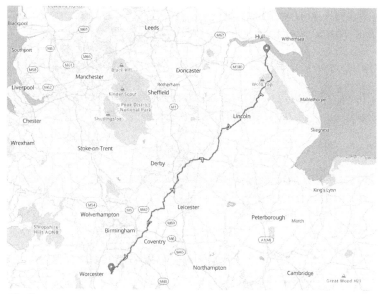

*Challenge 1*

# Chapter 4. Challenge One

The above is why I found myself at the Amicii kennels at 5am on the 3rd of June! It was colder than expected (6°C), so although it was expected to warm up later, I was wrapped up in arm warmers, leg warmers and just about all the clothes I had brought with me.

Still shivering with the cold, we did a short video for the Amicii Facebook page explaining what I was doing and why. I struggled to remain comprehensible under the circumstances, but I must have made some sense, judging my the reactions. Then that was it, I was off.

Prior to leaving I started the app that I'd downloaded on to my phone that in theory was going to allow people to follow my progress online. I'd tried it out on some training rides and it seemed pretty good – giving current location and speed, plus a small amount of recent history so it was possible to see the route I'd taken. I knew it was power-hungry, so I also took a couple of spare battery packs. A lot of faff to go to, but I thought it would be worth it in the long-run, as it would permit a little more "audience participation", as it were. I don't know – hasn't cycling become complicated!

I had plotted a route to Immingham some days earlier, as direct as possible, but avoiding as many main roads as I could. The application I used is designed to favour cycle routes and cycle-friendly roads and I have a cycle computer, so it's just a case of uploading the route, pressing "play" and following the prompts. Mostly. More on that later…

It quickly became obvious that navigation wasn't going to be the biggest issue during the ride. No, that was going to be the wind. The weather data for that day shows the wind was a steady 10 mph from the North-East, exactly the direction I was heading. Initially this wasn't such of a problem, as my route wound through the lanes of Worcestershire and Warwickshire, but as the day progressed in to the flatter counties of the east of England it became tedious, to say the least.

I followed the GPS prompts as they led me away from the kennels in to the Worcestershire countryside. Some of the roads were familiar, as I occasionally rode out this way from home to cafe stops as far afield as Warwick. Also, one of the Audax events I had recently ridden had a coffee stop in Atherstone and I had planned this as my first scheduled stop. That was at 40 miles though, a quarter of the way in to the total distance of 160 miles. It would take me three hours or so to get there though, so I couldn't just jump on the bike, ride for three hours and stop for breakfast. I shall explain (skip the next couple of paragraphs if you find it boring):

The NHS recommended calorie intake for women is 2000 calories/day, for men, 2500. That assumes a normal activity level. Calorie intake is calculated on your Basal Metabolic Rate (BMR), which is the amount of calories your body consumes at rest just being alive; plus active calories. Moderate cycling consumes about 400 calories/hour, so in order to maintain balance, I'd have to consume about 1200 calories even before breakfast! Additionally, it's necessary to maintain hydration. British Cycling suggest that even in cooler conditions aim to take on 500-750 ml per hour.

What I *try* to do, is take a small drink from my water bottle (bidon) as frequently as possible and eat every hour. In practice, I'm hopeless at both of these. I tend to take food I can eat while riding (bananas, flapjacks, nuts, gels, etc) then forget about it until all of a sudden I feel like I'm running out of energy, by which time it's a bit late. This phenomenon is called "bonking", in cycling parlance and hypoglycaemia in medical terms. It means you haven't consumed enough carbohydrates and allowed your blood sugar levels to drop too low. In an ideal world, you'd consume enough as you're riding along to prevent this happening, but as we all know, we don't live in an idea world, and I'm far from an ideal cyclist!

The first 40 miles, or ¼ of the route, to Atherstone was pretty much the hilliest. In total I think there was about 2000 metres (6,500 feet) of "up" to ride in total, but there was obviously a corresponding amount of "down" and nothing that could be construed as a serious climb. I grew up in West Somerset and a lot of my cycling as a youth had been undertaken in the Blackdown Hills, the Brendon Hills and Exmoor, so I've had plenty of experience on that front.

It wasn't long before I'd passed through a whole bunch of little villages, skirting to the south of larger places, Redditch, Solihull and Birmingham. I rode through Meriden, traditionally described as "the centre of England" and home to the Cyclists War Memorial, an obelisk dedicated to the cyclists killed in the First World War. Ten miles further on and I arrived at my breakfast stop, Atherstone! It was only 9 o'clock, so just over 3 hours for 25% of the way, I was happy with that. I didn't feel too bad and more importantly I felt even better after a full English breakfast!

After breakfast, I sat in the Market Square and made a quick progress video and sent it off to Ann, who was dealing with the social media aspects of the challenge. By this time the sun had well and truly got his hat on and it was about 18°C, so I stripped off a few of the layers I'd been wearing and set off across the cobbles towards Leicestershire.

Now, I've always been a bit interested in the study of the origin of words, or etymology and I was soon wondering about the origin of the names of "Sheepy

Magna" and "Sheepy Parva", as I rode through them. You'll be ecstatic to hear that I've had the opportunity to perform some research in to their toponymy and Nottingham University reliably informs me:

Sheepy Magna and Parva

'Sheep island'.
Elements and their meanings
scēp (Anglian) A sheep.
ēg (Anglian) An island. In ancient settlement-names, most frequently refers to dry ground surrounded by marsh. Also used of islands in modern sense. In late Old English names: well-watered land.
magna (Latin) Big, great.
parva (Latin) Small.


So, Sheepy Magna: Big Sheep Island. Sheepy Parva: Small Sheep Island. Every day's a school day.

Sheepy digressions aside, I continued through Market Bosworth and Coalville, after which I descended a huge hill and dropped down to the Leicestershire Wolds and from here for the next 80 miles or so was going to be mostly flat. With a headwind.

From Coalville I then went through Shepshed (more sheep), past Loughborough to Kingston on Soar. From there you can't fail to notice the massive power station at Ratcliffe-on-Soar with its eight massive cooling towers. This is a coal-fired power station, the last remaining in the UK, due to close in 2024.

Shortly afterwards, I passed through the village of Gotham… That had me wondering about Batman. Allegedly there is a link. I'll let you search for that one though.

My route took me through Nottingham, which I wasn't relishing. I don't like cycling in towns and cities, especially large ones and with a wider population of over ¾ of a million people, I don't think anyone could argue that Nottingham isn't large. In the event, it seems that my cycle-route planning had done a pretty good job and I made my way through the south of the city on a range of quiet roads, back-streets and cycle paths. The only fly in the ointment was the trams. Tram tracks and bicycle wheels don't mix and I was particularly careful to ensure that mine didn't.

Before I knew it, I'd traversed Nottingham and stopped for lunch in a place called Radcliffe on Trent. I did quite like the look of the Italian restaurant, but considered that while it might be nice, it would probably introduce too much delay in to the proceedings. A perpetual choice: eat proper food, or get a move on! I chose the latter and settled for a sausage roll and some cake from the baker next door and sat on a bench outside in the sun. Given that it had also warmed up somewhat, I bought a couple of bottles of "sports drink" from the supermarket over the road. My bidons were long-since empty and needed refilling.

Before continuing I made another progress video for Ann to upload. By this time we'd already met my original fundraising target of £500, which was truly amazing and for some inexplicable reason I decided to offer a "double or quits" challenge and said that if we managed to raise £1000, I would ride back from Immingham to Worcester the following day! To be honest, I hadn't actually planned how I would get back. One option was for Jill to come and collect me in the car, another was to take a train. Cycling back most definitely wasn't an option I'd considered.

With that bombshell dropped, I headed out of Radcliffe towards the east. Eighty miles down, eighty to go! I negotiated the A46 Bingham Interchange via a very useful cycle path and bridge and headed through Bingham before arriving in a little village called Aslockton. Now, for some reason my GPS had a bit of a "moment" here. "Turn left!" it said. I turned left. "Off course!" it said. Oh. I turned around and went back. "Course found!" it said. Great, I think, and headed off down the road. "Off course!" it bleeped at me. What? Really? There followed a series of toing and froing with an associated series of bleeps, not all from the GPS! I even stopped to ask someone for directions once. Imagine that. A man asking for directions. Unfortunately the person I asked wasn't local and couldn't help. Don't say I didn't try! Then, almost as suddenly as it had started, the bleeping stopped and normal route guidance was resumed. No idea what caused it to this day. Ripples in the space-time continuum, perhaps.

A few miles further on, I was directed on to the Newark to Cotham sustrans cycle path, which follows the trackbed of the old Newark to Bottesford railway. Old railways make great cycle routes and this one was no exception. They are fairly flat and this one was even surfaced in parts. It took me straight in to the centre of Newark on Trent, as it ends at the current railway station. From there, I picked up route 64 of the National Cycle Network, which took me out of Newark towards Lincoln. I didn't stay on route 64 though, as while it might have been very pretty as it wound its way through the lanes, yet again time was of concern. I opted to head across to the A46, which although sounds like it might be a cycling nightmare, fortunately has a reasonable cycle path to one side and as it was built along the Fosse Way, was straight as a die and went directly in to Lincoln.

Now, Lincoln was my 75% marker, ¾ of the way to Immingham. After I'd struggled up the massive hill to the cathedral (who put that there?) I sat on a bench and surveyed the battery level on my phone, which was deep in to the red. There was no way I was going to be able to record another video and unfortunately I had to stop the tracking app. I had plugged in a backup battery, but the app was draining the phone as fast as the battery was charging it. A shame, but unfortunately I needed my phone in case of emergencies more than I needed the tracking app. A little further down the road I pulled in to a coffee shop for my last "meal" of the ride. It was hot now too and while I was inside downing a large latte and numerous cakes, the temperature sensor on my GPS recorded

36°C. It was in full sun though, but without a shadow of a doubt, even at 4pm, it was still hot.

From Lincoln, I unwittingly picked up the EuroVelo 12 "North Sea Cycle Route". EuroVelo is a network of 17 long-distance cycle routes that cross and connect Europe, a concept that was implemented by the European Cyclists' Federation, the European umbrella federation of civil society organisations advocating and working for more and better cycling. I didn't really think about it at the time, but EuroVelo in a way was to become a much larger factor in my not-so-distant future.

The flat terrain of Lincolnshire continued, as did the headwind, and the low hedges didn't offer much respite here. One saving factor was that as the hours wore on, the temperature began to drop at last. My legs were tired now though and I was beginning to wish it would all stop!

I knew I had one final challenge to overcome though; The Lincolnshire Wolds. These are a range of low hills running parallel to the coast of the North Sea and while they could never be described as mountains, the hill at Walesby rises nearly 400 feet in a little over a mile and a half. I rolled through the village, psychologically preparing myself as best as possible, but my heart still sank a little when I rounded the corner at the bottom and saw the hill in front of me. There was nothing for it, I dropped the gears down and down until there were none left and ground up slowly in bottom gear. After churning away in my "granny gear" for what seemed like eternity, I finally crested what I thought was the top of the hill, only to be confronted after a short downhill section with a (fortunately somewhat shorter) climb to the actual summit. To put this in to some kind of context, the "King of the Mountains" on this particular hill (Ethan Hayter of Ineos Grenadiers) completed the climb in 4 minutes 13 seconds. I am currently in 2,681st place with 11 minutes 35 seconds. I don't think I'm going to be troubling the starting line of the Tour de France any time soon!

It was now 6.15pm and I'd been cycling for 13 hours. I had 17 miles to go and it was all downhill wasn't it? Should be a breeze from here, surely? No, it wasn't. The road did drop down again, but then turned north along the undulating Wolds, to the East of Grimsby. I kept thinking to myself, "I can't be that far from the sea – surely I should see the coast soon". I pushed on and on, looking at the distance on my GPS, looking towards the east – nothing.

Finally, as I dropped down towards the village of Limber, I saw a first glimpse of the Humber Estuary and the industrial areas that run along the south coast. Fourteen hours in to the ride, I had my first sight of Immingham! I quickly made a video update and sent it off to Ann. Seven miles to go!

I put in a final spurt of effort. Effort always seems to come a little easier when the end it in sight – that, and it was now truly all downhill to the finish. I passed through the final villages of Brocklesby and Habrough and I was on the final stretch in to South Killingholme, location of the Immingham kennels. I wasn't sure who would even be there now – it was gone 7.30pm and I thought they might all have given up and gone home, but no – I could see someone in the distance! My reception committee (Kelly) took the final video as I rolled up to the kennels at 7.34pm! I was shattered. So much so, I think I nearly fell over as I stopped pedalling and got off the bike. I'd cycled 160.4 miles in 14 hours and 21 minutes and I felt at the time like it had been one of the hardest things I'd ever done. We had raised £761 for Amicii though and that was enough to have made it worthwhile. It was £261 more than my original goal and what's more, I think I breathed a quiet sigh of relief that we hadn't hit £1,000, as that meant I didn't have to cycle back!

# CHAPTER 5. CHALLENGE ONE, AGAIN?

Or should that be challenge two? Or at least challenge 1a? I'd made it from Worcester to Immingham anyway, that was enough for now. I was tired and aching and probably didn't smell very nice either. I'd arranged to meet my cousin near Grimsby, who'd kindly offered to put me up for the night and make me some dinner. Her reputation as an exceptional cook preceded her, I just hoped that she hadn't given up on me due to my late arrival. Luckily that was not the case and despite it being gone 8pm she was still waiting for me.

First things first though, I had a shower and changed in to some lightweight shorts and a tee shirt I'd brought with me. We then sat down to the most amazing steak pie and mash that she'd prepared for me, all polished off with a nice glass of cider! We sat and talked in to the night, discussing family matters and putting the world to rights, but I think I may have started nodding off at times, I was so tired. At some stage I must have made my excuses and headed off to bed.

I slept well, but I awoke with a start. Normally I wake with a big furry nose poking me, telling me it's time for walkies. This usually happens at about 5am, so technically at 6am Stella would have let me have a lie-in!

My phone had been busy during the night. I had received many emails from JustGiving and even more notifications from Facebook.

The first thing I did was check on my JustGiving page. Oh dear. £1,050. Never one to renege on a promise, I opened Messenger:

*Me: Morning Kelly. Any chance of a lift? Looks like I've got a bike ride to do?*

*Kelly: Of course, what time?*

*Me: Nobody awake here, so not sure what time they will get up. Oh, hang on… When can you come over? Just going to have a cuppa*

*Kelly: About 1/2 an hour OK ?*

*Me: Brilliant!*

I sent Ann a message too, to let her know.

*Ann: Are you really going to ride back?*

*Me: Yep*

*Ann: Blimey… OK so I will put up a post this morning. I can't quite believe you're doing it, but good on you!*

So, after a couple of pieces of toast and a cup of tea, I was back at Immingham kennels ready to do the whole thing again in reverse! Yet again, Kelly made a short video so we could update Facebook, and at 7.46am, I pushed the pedals and set off again.

Yesterday's north-easterly was still with me, but whereas yesterday I'd struggled to ride in to it all day, today, it was at my back. I felt a bit stiff as I set off, but as I got a little further and started to warm up, the stiffness eased and with the tailwind everything was set.

The pie and mash of the previous night had obviously done me the world of good, because climbing back up on to the Wolds didn't seem anything like as gruelling as it had the previous day. That's probably more to do with the fact that the climb is longer and less steep, rather than the short, sharp rise at Walesby. I flew across the flat section from Market Rasen to Lincoln and indeed 2 hours and 40 minutes after leaving Immingham I'd ridden 40 miles and stopped in Lincoln for something to eat and drink.

Back on the road again after 20 minutes and I headed down the steep hill from Lincoln Cathedral. My GPS had a bit of a turn here, because basically all I had done was reversed the route. That was great, but unfortunately it didn't understand the concept of one-way streets and kept trying to send me the wrong way up them. I just kept ignoring it and went the way I thought I should be going. Eventually it all worked out OK.

The tailwind blew me across the flat Lincolnshire countryside and soon I was in Newark on Trent again. Along the disused railway in the other direction – don't get lost in Aslockton – then I stopped at Bingham for lunch at the 80 mile mark. "Lunch" consisted of a sandwich and a packet of crisps from a local shop that just happened to be open. Of course, because day two was a Sunday, there were fewer shops to choose from. I'd been gasping for a drink for a while and had looked out for somewhere in Newark on Trent to fill up my bidons, but I hadn't passed anywhere open that I'd noticed. By the time I got to Bingham it was also warming up. It was now 25°C and I should have drank a lot more than I had. I made a short video outside the shop in Bingham, but playing it back afterwards I'm not sure it made a lot of sense. I may have been suffering from heat-induced gobbledygook. As I sat in the sun, rather than finding some shade my GPS registered a temperature of 36°C.

Lunch dispensed with, I set off towards Nottingham again. Part of the cycle route runs through the village of Holme Pierrepoint and past the National Water Sports Centre. I didn't stop to do any canoeing or white-water rafting, but I did note that the state of the road was terrible, riddled as it was with potholes. I must have noticed it on the previous day too, but in my now tired and saddle-sore state it was much more of an issue. I tried to weave in and out of the potholes as much as possible, but sometimes my reactions just weren't fast enough and I rode straight through some, the shock jarring me to the bone.

I retraced my route back through Nottingham again without too much difficulty and avoiding any interaction with trams. Just as I was passing Clifton I caught up with another cyclist who was towing a trailer with a Staffordshire Bull Terrier in it. We chatted for a while and I wondered if Stella would perhaps like a trailer to ride in? Unlikely…

Back through Gotham, stopping to fill up with sports drink and chocolate yet again; through Kingston on Soar and past Loughborough. I stopped in a lay-by. I'd ridden 90 miles and I was shattered. I still had 70 miles to go and it was half past three. Had I bitten off more than I could chew? Just at that moment my phone pinged. It was Ann.

*Ann: If you need to be picked up at any time I'm ready to come and get you.*

*Me: I'm good.*

The truth was that I wasn't good. I was so tired…

*Ann: Good. Everyone is talking about you and how amazing you are! KEEP GOING… inspirational many people have said.*

Inspirational? I didn't feel very inspirational right then.

*Me: I'm near Loughborough. It's just so HOT!*

*Ann: I know. Awful.*

*Me: I could kill a 99*

*Ann: Ha ha that might be tricky to keep cold!*

*Me: It gets hillier from here too*

Right, I thought. I'm "inspirational". Best get a move on. I rummaged in my bag for the tube of chamois cream I'd bought with me and slapped a bit on. Things were getting a bit complicated down below and it couldn't make it any worse. Onward and upward. Literally.

Less than 15 minutes later I was in Shepshed again, stopped outside a supermarket. They didn't have a 99, but they did have ice-cream and yet more sports drink. I'm not sure the ice-cream would have helped my energy levels much, but it definitely helped morale.

From Shepshed towards Coalville the road rises 500 feet in about four miles. I was leaving the flat terrain of the east and the rest of the ride would be undulating.

On any other day this wouldn't have been a problem, but with 260 miles in my legs every uphill section meant I was down in to my granny gears again, making for really slow progress. I was mentally ticking off the place names now. My psychological goal wasn't the Worcester kennels, it was the next town. Hugglescote. Nearly got taken out by a car at the traffic lights, trying to overtake and then just pulling in on me. Ibstock. Might be able to get a drink at the Co-Op? No, closed. Market Bosworth. Is that shop open? No. Maybe a pub? Better not. I'd probably never leave again! Through the Sheepy's again. I don't think San Giovanni's Italian would appreciate a smelly cyclist turning up for dinner.

It was half-past five. Atherstone. There had to be somewhere open in Atherstone. There might well have been, but I didn't see it. I probably should have looked a little harder, but instead I sat on a bench and ate my last flapjack. That would have to do. I made another movie, trying to sound more upbeat than I felt. Only 40 miles to go now. Familiar roads.

Those miles passed in a hyperglycaemic haze. The flapjack helped, but I could have done with something more to be honest. I'm sure I could have found somewhere to stop and eat something, but I wasn't thinking straight. The end goal was in sight and I just wanted it all to be over. I kept finding hills that I didn't remember on the way out. I guess that's because they were downhill, not uphill.

I was getting closer now. I stopped to share a GPS tracking link with Ann, so she should see roughly when I might arrive at the kennels. I could have picked a better place than a shady lane near a stream, because as I fiddled away at my telephone I was gradually being eaten alive by mosquitoes.

The last hill of the day was conquered, from Sambourne to The Ridgeway. That was it. To all intents and purposes I was "home". I texted Ann to say I wouldn't be long. Those last ten miles flew by. The goal was in sight and I had found some deep-down energy reserves from somewhere. It felt like the final stage of the Tour de France to me as I flashed through Inkberrow, Worcestershire. I turned off the main road towards Flyford. All that remained now was a mile or so up a slight rise to the kennels. I could see the finish line – and the reception committee! It was 8.35pm, I'd been on the road for 12 hours and 49 minutes.

Ann was filming one final movie as I rolled up so I had to try and keep my remarks family-friendly, which I think I did pretty successfully. I gave my thanks to everyone that had supported me in the endeavour. It seemed as if so many people had been following me along the road, commenting on Ann and my posts. I didn't get a chance to read them all as I rode alone, but looking back on them in retrospect all of them were truly motivational and caring. I couldn't have gone the distance if it hadn't have been for the help of the Amicii team, most of all Captain Ann! All I did was ride a bike.

The day after, I made the following post on Facebook:

*Morning all! Just downloaded the data from my GPS this morning and it's revealed some interesting (yawn) facts...*

*- It took nearly an hour longer on Saturday than the ride back on Sunday due to the headwind.*

*- I rode 2 miles further on Saturday than on Sunday, because I got lost in Aslockton.*

*- While I sat outside the shop in Bingham on Sunday having some lunch, my GPS recorded 38°C!*

*- Most of all, we learnt how generous everybody is, so please accept my gratitude for all your donations and all the lovely comments along the way.*

*Now... How far is it from Viișoara to Worcester?*

In all, we raised £1,504 for Amicii.

# CHAPTER 6. UNFINISHED WORK

A couple of months passed since my ride and I'd been busy. I'd recently changed job and moved house, so most of June was spent packing and most of July unpacking. I had been out on my bike a couple of times in June, but not at all in July. We'd also been on holiday in July, Interrailing around Europe visiting a whole host of cities; Brussels, Vienna, Budapest, Brno, Prague, Berlin, Cologne. You'd think I'd have been done with travelling, but no, something was missing…

It was that last throwaway comment I'd made on my Facebook post, "How far is it from Viișoara to Worcester?" It's 1,700 miles, that's how far it is.

To the unfamiliar, Viișoara is the town in Romania where Amicii has its rescue kennels. It's home to around 300 dogs, cats and a donkey, that have either been rescued from the streets, or abandoned at the shelter. It's run by a dedicated team of volunteers, headed up by Dora, who began rescuing strays in 2000. In her own words, "What motivates me? What kept me continuing when everybody said this is suicide and I should run away from this story too? It is not just the love for the strays! It is a much more noble and pure feeling! It is Compassion! Because suffering is unnecessary, animals do not need to suffer, but we humans do, we can learn from suffering and pain, it can make us better and more pure, but they do not need to, they are already pure and innocent in the deepest meaning of the word. Their suffering is useless and meaningless and that is why I dedicate my life to rescue and dream continuously of a world when I will not need to any more."

The question remained though, in my head, if in nobody else's, could I ride my bike from the Amicii kennels in Viișoara, to the Amicii kennels in Worcestershire? One Thousand, Seven Hundred miles. That was some undertaking. I'd ridden 950 miles from Land's End to John O'Groats, but that was in 2014 and I was a lot fitter.

Then there was the question of time. LEJOG had taken me 11 days, an average of 85 miles/day. If I could only get two weeks holiday, that was 16 days and I'd have to average over 100 miles/day. I started doing the sums. I'd have to fly to Cluj-Napoca, the closest I could get to Viișoara, which is still about 30 miles away. I can ride that, no problem. Then I discovered that flights to Cluj-Napoca only go twice a week and the flight on Saturday actually arrives at 1.45am on Sunday morning. Unless I was going to cycle to Viișoara in the dark I was going to have to stay in Cluj until daylight, then ride to Viișoara, so I'd pretty much lose two days even before I started. It was looking less and less possible the more I looked at it.

It was time for another conversation with Ann.

*Me: Hi Ann  - When is is the next happy bus going to Romania please?*

*Ann: September 14*

*Me: Interesting...*

*Ann: Why?*

*Me: Would there be space for a bicycle?*

*Ann: Yes of course. What are you thinking?? I'm imagining your reply…*

*Ann: Options are:*

*1) it's a donation*

*2) I'm going to cycle from Romania to the U.K.*

*Me: 2.*

*Ann: You're nuts*

Well. That wasn't quite the reaction I expected. It did however force a timescale on to the plan. It was the 17th of August. If I was going to do this, I had a month to prepare.

Firstly, I had to put in for leave. I didn't know how that was going to go. I'd only been with the company four months. With my tongue well and truly in my cheek I applied for three weeks leave. I didn't have any more and if it did get approved it meant I wouldn't be able to take any time off over Christmas. Perhaps if I did manage to ride back in less time I could claim some of it back anyway?

A few days later my leave request came back. Approved! I messaged Ann.

*Me: I have booked holiday from 18 September*

*Ann: Omg really you are going to do this?*

*Me: Do you think I shouldn't?*

*Ann: It's up to you! It's just a massive thing and we can try to provide as much help and support as possible*

The wheels were very much in motion.

There is a well-known proverb, "A journey of a thousand miles begins with a single step", but it's often that first step that is the most difficult. Once you have taken that step, hopefully everything else falls in to order. I had to make a plan, because although I'd made the commitment, I still didn't have one. Sure, I had a rough outline, but it needed fleshing out.

The rough outline consisted of "give bike to Ann to take to Romania; fly out there to meet it; cycle 100 miles/day for 17 days, taking the ferry from Hook of Holland to Harwich; go home".

I couldn't use the same bike that I had used in challenge one – it was too much of a lightweight, with skinny tyres and an aluminium frame. I did have a more suitable bike though, one of the advantages of having "too many bikes", I guess. This was an old, steel-framed touring bike I'd bought second-hand several years ago. That would do the job nicely. It was still languishing in my daughter's garage though, where I'd stored it while we were moving house. I brought it back to our house; It was very dusty and covered in cobwebs, but after I'd thrown a bucket of soapy water over it, it looked OK. It would have to do.

What I was going to take depended very much on where I was going to stay. I didn't really want to stay in hotels, as they were too expensive. If I spent too much money I felt I might as well just give the money to Amicii and stay at home. That left Airbnb and camping. Finally, there was the option of couch surfing, an option offered by several websites, such as warmshowers and bewelcome. I mulled this over with Jill and eventually decided to prepare for all eventualities. This meant I had to take my camping gear and panniers, which had been in a box in the attic for a few years. I hoped they were still all OK!

I thought it would also be a good idea to ramp up the miles on the bike too. I had done nothing in July at all and yet here I was proposing to cycle 1,700 miles! I was back to the 100 miles/day target. I knew I could ride 100 miles in a day – after all, the previous Amicii challenge had been 320 miles in two days, but I was shattered after that. What was an unknown factor was whether I could ride 100 miles, then get up the next day and ride another 100 miles. Then another and another…

The first weekend in August I managed 40 miles in the pouring rain. Then a couple of rides in the evenings – only twenty-odd miles or so each, but time was limited by working during the day and walking dogs in the morning and evening too. The second weekend I couldn't ride as it was my sister's birthday and I had to drive to Somerset for that. More evening rides, then a 100 mile ride at the weekend. Bank holiday Monday saw another 100 mile ride, then the following weekend saw a 200km (128 mile) Audax, which I rode on my touring bike as a "shake-down" exercise.

The 9th of September was the Amicii dog show, which I'd chosen as the official launch date of my ride. Up until then, only a select few knew about it. I set up my stand at the village hall in Welland in an attempt to convey the concept of the ride to all and sundry. I had decided to call this trip "Stella's Journey", as it was a symbolic retracing of the trip that she had taken from Romania to the United Kingdom.

In parallel with all this, there was a considerable amount of activity from the Amicii team. Captain Ann had swung in to action, organizing things so that the van could take my bike to Viișoara, instead of me having to pack it in a box for the flight. I'd set up a new JustGiving page and a blog for those that aren't on Facebook. My daughter set up a TikTok page that she was going to manage. The idea was that I was going to send updates to a group chat and/or post them publicly to Facebook and the team were going to take media from there and share on various social media channels. Ann had spoken to some of the local media, hoping to publicise the trip as much as possible. We were going all-out, or so it seemed!

The 13th of September saw me dropping off my bike at Ann's for onward transport to Romania. I did wonder if I'd ever see it again. It crossed my mind that if I did arrive in Romania and it wasn't there, what would my options be? I would have my luggage with me, so I guess I could buy a bike locally? I put these thoughts out of my head. Of course my bike would be there!

My flight was booked for the 16th of September in the evening, which left me room to spend some time with Jill and Stella. I did feel guilty about leaving Jill for up to three weeks to deal with Stella and our two other dogs, Dizzy and Lucy. It's not like I didn't have her blessing though. We had discussed the whole thing in depth. Jill said it's irrelevant what she says as I'll do what I like anyway. I saw that as a blessing.

Ann swung by my house in the afternoon to drop off some Amicii tee shirts for me and the team in Romania and to record a quick video and then I was ready to go. I loaded all my panniers in to the car and we set off for Birmingham airport. There wasn't any need for long goodbyes at the airport, so Jill unceremoniously left me at the drop-off point with a pile of luggage and drove off. I had plenty of time, so I strolled down to the terminal with my bags, pausing only to take a quick photo outside. Inside there didn't appear to be anywhere to sit and grab a coffee, as there seemed to be some kind of remodelling going on. Instead I hung around next to the WizzAir departure area, waiting for somebody to check in my luggage.

I had two panniers and a handlebar bag with me and as with all budget airlines I had to pay extra for baggage. One pannier would go in the hold, the other and the handlebar bag in the cabin. I had to take my one pannier to "oversized luggage", not because it was particularly large, but because it was soft-shelled and had straps. It didn't seem to make any difference though, because it went on the same conveyor as all the rest of the baggage. I went upstairs to departures, through passport control and to security. This was where things became more complicated, as the man at the x-ray machine kept rejecting my bags due to unidentifiable liquids.

Security: "What's that then?"
Me: "Chamois cream"
Security: "What's that for?"
Me: "Chafing"
Security: "Chafing?"
Me: "Yes. I'm cycling back from Romania"
Security: "Oh wow! Good luck…"

With that, I was allowed to go. I joined the throng of passengers in the departure lounge. I'm not sure, but I think I may have been the only non-Romanian passenger there. Eventually, it was time to board. The crew decided they were going to board the plane by seat row numbers, starting at the back. My seat number was 1F, so I imagined I might have a long wait. Utter chaos then reigned, as the man at the gate kept repeating, "only rows… to …". This continued for quite a while, until he gave up and it became a free-for-all. Eventually everyone was on board, the door was closed, the safety briefing was undertaken and the wheels left the ground. Romania here I come!

*No going back now!*

# Chapter 7. Romania

## Day 1, Viișoara to Aiud

31 miles.

We touched-down in Cluj-Napoca at about 2am local time, cleared customs pretty quickly, went to retrieve my extra pannier from the luggage carousel and walked out in to arrivals. I'd booked an Airbnb pretty close to the airport where I could get my head down for a few hours, before setting off towards Viișoara. It was only a mile or so away and to be honest I could have walked, but at 2am in an unfamiliar city I opted for a taxi instead. I can't remember how much I paid now, but I remember thinking to myself that the price was a bit steep, so I tried to knock him down. He made an excuse, saying he had to pay for the parking. I said I'd walk and headed off, but he gave me a lower (but still expensive) price, which I accepted. I threw my bags in the boot and we shot off down the road. I gave him the address and by the time he'd put it in his phone, we'd actually overshot the destination, it was that close! He had to turn around and drive back.

The taxi driver deposited me and my luggage out side an ordinary looking low-rise apartment block. I fumbled with my phone, looking for the information the host had sent me. I had to walk down the side of the block, find a key box, enter the code and let myself in to the building. Then climb the stairs to the 3$^{rd}$ floor and let myself in to the apartment. The instructions were very detailed, including pictures, but I wandered up and down outside the building for a while, unable to find the key box. I eventually used the torch app on my phone to shed some light on the matter and with that, I found the key box. Shortly afterwards, I was in my apartment for the night, bags in a pile, asleep on the bed. I didn't sleep particularly well and awoke fairly early. I guess it was a combination of things – strange location, excitement, etc.

I planned on taking the train from Cluj-Est to Câmpia Turzii, the closest station to  Viișoara. There was a train at 7.56am, which I didn't think I'd be able to catch, after such a short sleep. I'd booked the 11:44 train instead, thinking I'd be able to have a nice long snooze and a leisurely breakfast. In the event, I probably could have taken the earlier train, as I slept so fitfully it wouldn't have made much difference.

Still, it was Sunday morning and I had plenty of time. I arose, had a shower and ate one of my porridge sachets for breakfast, with a cup of coffee. I still had plenty of time, as the station was only 5 minutes walk from the apartment. I decided to go for a stroll to the local supermarket, "Mega Image", which I could see from the window. They did a pretty good line of pastries, so I bought an apple strudel.

As I wandered back to the apartment, a little black and white stray dog walked up to me. Ann had told me this was likely to happen. He seemed like a friendly chap, although he had a bit of a gammy leg and a few fleas. I shared some apple strudel with him, for which he seemed very grateful. I couldn't do much more.

Back at the apartment, I gathered my bags together and readied myself to leave. Check and double-check I had everything with me, as I was required to post the keys in to the letterbox, after which I would let myself out and be unable to re-enter.

I walked down the road again and across the railway tracks. I'm not sure if it was an approved crossing or not, but it seemed like it was reasonably well-used. As stepped across the rails, I admired the old UAZ-452 "Bushanka" van, which had been adapted to run on the rails. I don't know whether that was a factory option or not?

A few minutes later and I was at a deserted Cluj-Napoca Est railway station. There wasn't much in the way of facilities, although there was a waiting room (also deserted). Not sure what I was expecting – a Costa coffee shop? I might of expected a platform, maybe, but there didn't seem to be one.

A few minutes later, a train approached the station, but I didn't think it could be mine, as it was far too early and was wearing the livery of OBB (Österreichische Bundesbahnen), the Austrian railways. I was waiting for a CFR Călători (Căile Ferate Române) train. The OBB train did stop at the station though, which boded well. Nobody got on or off, but a smartly dressed Stationmaster appeared from Cluj-Est station and stood to attention, before waving the train off.

Almost at 11:44 to the dot, a blue  CFR Călători train appeared in the distance, trundled slowly in to the station and stopped. The Stationmaster appeared again, as if by magic. I was still the only person in the station (apart from the  Stationmaster), so I walked across the tracks and boarded. The Stationmaster waved his flag and the train set off.

The train was one of those that have an upstairs and a downstairs, with first class on the top floor. I'd bought a first class ticket, as I thought the few extra pennies was probably worthwhile. I clambered up the stairs to an almost empty carriage, dumped my bags on the floor and took a seat next to the window. Shortly after, a ticket inspector appeared, so I showed him the QR code on my phone, with which he appeared to be satisfied. "Câmpia Turzii?" I enquired. "Yes", he replied. At least I was on the correct train.

The journey was going to take about an hour, with stops at Dezmir, Apahida, Cojocna, Tunel, Boju, Valea Florilor, Ploscoșa and Cânepiști. I'd looked at the route on Google maps prior to leaving the UK, as I had investigated the possibility of cycling from Cluj-Napoca to  Viișoara. The options were either the E81 dual-carriageway which I didn't fancy much, or a lot of unsurfaced tracks. The railway cut through the countryside in a more-or-less direct route, so I chose the easy option.

The easy option also appeared to be the most picturesque, as the train wound its way through the hills of Cluj county, past fields of maize and sunflowers, crossing rivers and streams. Each time we stopped at a station, the smartly-uniformed Stationmaster would appear to greet us and wave us off, despite there sometimes being no passengers alighting.

The train arrived in Câmpia Turzii at 12.47pm, bang on time. Dora had arranged for Gicu to collect me and as I walked out through the station doors, there he was. I would have been instantly recognizable, as I was wearing my Amicii tee shirt. We walked over to his van, where we quickly established that he didn't speak much English and I spoke no Romanian whatsoever. However, we did discover that we both spoke Spanish, so we managed to chat. In fact, I found myself communicating in Spanish quite a lot in

Romania – it seemed a fairly common spoken language.

From the station we drove to Dora's mother's house, where my bike had been delivered late the previous evening. To my relief, everything was present and correct. I shouldn't have doubted it for a minute. We squeezed the bike in the back of the van and set off for the shelter, a few minutes away in the countryside outside Viișoara.

You could tell when we arrived. With approximately 300 dogs in rescue, there was a lot of barking! I was met at the gate by Dora, Daniela and Ioana, who had given up their Sunday to volunteer at the kennels. Not just today, but every day. We unloaded my bike and bags and took them inside, where the ladies had laid on some food they'd saved from a previous wedding! I wasn't expecting lunch, but here were sandwiches, cake and even beer! I thought it wouldn't be wise to partake in too much beer, as I was expecting to cycle at least some part of my route today. Dora also presented me with a (small) bottle of "Victory" brandy and some chocolate, which I promised not to drink until I had reached the end of my journey. I would very much have liked to stay an extra night in Viișoara with the team, but I was pressured by time and felt like I had to move on.

I couldn't leave without seeing the dogs though. After all, it was all about the dogs. Daniela led me around the hillside in the sunshine, meeting them all. I felt a little overwhelmed as we walked around the rows and rows of kennels. Daniela introduced me to all the dogs, one-by-one. Some were bouncy and friendly, some were scared and hid in the back of their kennels and some were scared and aggressive. All of them were cared for with love and dedication of the Amicii team. Speaking to Dora afterwards, I could see the tears welling up in her eyes. That started me off too. Dora knows that not all of the dogs in the shelter can look forward to a forever home, as some of them just haven't had the right start in life. Nevertheless, the alternatives are just not feasible, so those that can't be re-homed will live out their lives in the shelter, cared for by Dora and her team.

It was time to make a move. It was now mid-afternoon and if I was going to make a start on my ride, I needed to do it sooner rather than later. I made my way back to the cabin to get changed in to my cycling gear. I rolled up my shorts and tee shirt and put them away in my pannier. These were the only non-cycling clothes I had and they would need to see me through the next three weeks. I attached my panniers to my bike and wheeled it out of the shelter. One final hug from the ladies, a quick movie for Facebook and I was off. I wobbled down the road from the shelter towards Viișoara, the sound of good wishes ringing in my ears. I was unused to the extra weight of camping gear and panniers and it would take some time to become accustomed to it.

As before, I'd worked out my route in advance, using a bike routing website. I'd told it to plot a route from Viișoara to Hook of Holland, then taken that route and split it in to 100 mile chunks. Each one of those chunks was intended to be one day's ride. I'd been back over each section time and time again using Google satellite view and Google street view to try and make sure the route was appropriate. I tried to re-plot the route away from main roads and dual-carriageways wherever possible, or at least minimize those sections. I also tried to use cycle routes where possible and I was surprised to see that there was even one cycle route in Romania that appeared on OpenStreetMap. My first day's cycling was supposed to be from Viișoara to the city of Deva. That was supposing I'd set off early in the morning though, not at half-past three in the afternoon. There was no way I would make Deva today. Instead, Dora thought Aiud might be a more realistic goal, some 30 miles distant. I had also originally planned to head south from Câmpia Turzii to pick up the "cycle route" at Ocna Mureș, then ride the quiet roads south of the river Mureș (pronounced "mur-esh"). However, I wanted to buy some methylated spirits for my Trangia stove and I'd discovered that the most likely place I would be able to buy this was a store called "Dedeman" in

Turda, eight miles to the west. Amazing what you can discover from the comfort of your own home…

So, I headed west out of Câmpia Turzii on the DN15, which although was a fairly major road, was pretty quiet on a Sunday afternoon. After a minor navigational error, which saw me in the Lidl car park instead of on the road (but fortunately made me avoid the underpass), I was out of town and soon in the outskirts of Turda. I'd plotted my route so that my GPS took me straight to Dedeman's front door, arriving at 4pm. Luckily, Sunday trading hours in Romania seem to be more liberal than in the UK, as the store was open until 6pm. I locked my bike outside, although I wasn't 100% comfortable leaving my bike and all my luggage unattended, walked inside and asked the nearest staff member for "Alcool metilic". My pronunciation must have been OK, because we rushed off through the maze of aisles and shortly later I was proudly presenting my Alcool metilic at the cashier. She didn't ask me if I was over 18 or anything and my Google pay went "ping", so we were all good! Outside, I poured the meths in to my Trangia bottle, tucked it away in my pannier and that was mission accomplished.

I headed south out of Turda on the "Strada 22 Decembrie 1989", which the more mature of my readers will recognise as the date of the Romanian revolution, ending the communist regime of Nicolae

Ceaușescu. I stopped at the junction of the 22$^{nd}$ of December and the E81 at a Lukoil petrol station to grab a bottle of water (Aqua Carpatica was going to become a regular for me over the next few days) and an ice-cream. I then had a fraught couple of miles as the E81 was the link road between Turda and the A3 motorway and hence was very busy with cars and lorries. Unfortunately there was no alternative and the next mile or so was quite scary, especially as the E81 crossed the A3 and there was no pavement, no shoulder, nothing. I kept as close to the side as I could and to be honest, the truck drivers gave me as wide a berth as they could, oncoming traffic permitting. Nevertheless, I was glad when I reached the junction of the A3 and – as I had hoped – the majority of the traffic turned on to the motorway, leaving the E81 almost empty.

Almost immediately after the junction I was treated to the first hill of the trip. It was only a couple of hundred feet in elevation, but with the extra weight on board I just sat in the saddle, changed down a few gears and took it easy. The route I'd plotted didn't have a huge amount of hills in it, not yet, anyway. Once I'd met up with the Mureș river at Unirea, I would follow the Mureș valley all the way to Arad, indeed, all the way to Szeged in Hungary. As a rule, rivers don't tend to flow uphill and I could look forward to a few days of riding mostly downhill!

I could see the motorway to my right, as it ran pretty much parallel to my route all the way to Deva, where it veered off to the south towards Timișoara. A few miles down the road I passed from Cluj county in to Alba county and continued through the rolling hills. There were a few rest areas and even some disused hotels, as prior to the construction of the motorway, this was obviously the main road. Now it had become the "old road", it was much more enjoyable. I stopped at a rest area near Dumbrava, overlooking the impressive "Mănăstirea Dumbrava", or the Monastery of St. Great Martyr Demetrios. I sat and enjoyed a drink and something to eat as I admired the monastery in the distance, then made a quick video to upload to our group chat. It's only now as I write this, that I discover that the monastery was only built in the last 30 years, being consecrated in 1998.

At that time, I was still aiming for Alba Iulia, which would have been about 60 miles for the day, but as the day wore on, reality began to set in and I had to admit that Dora was correct and Aiud was a more practical target for the day. This was only another 10 or 12 miles further on from Dumbrava and I rolled in to town about 6pm. My original GPS route would have taken me across the river again here, so I turned off navigation before it started chirping at me about being off course and proceeded towards the city centre. It's not a large city by any standards, with a population of only 21,000. That undoubtedly explains why Google didn't have a lot to offer me under accommodation. I'd already passed one guest house and I didn't fancy back-tracking, so I found myself at the door of the Hotel Magnolia. I left my bike outside and entered the rather grand looking entrance hall. It looked as if there was some kind of party in progress as well, as there was a banqueting hall full of people.

I found a lady to ask about a room and everything seemed OK, but when I asked if there was somewhere safe I could leave my bike, she replied with a firm "No". I wasn't about to leave my bike on the pavement so I said I'd go and check out the nearby Hotel Victoria. "That's closed", she said. Things weren't looking so good and it looked as if I might have to continue on my way, or camp by the roadside. Finally she said "you could put your bike in the room", so that was settled. I paid my 150 Lei and was shown to my room.

Given the splendour of the entrance and the banqueting hall, I was possibly expecting more, but after I'd been led up a marble staircase, we entered a long corridor off of which was my room. The room could be described as "basic", at best. Still, beggars can't be choosy. The bed linen was clean and the water was hot. It would do.

I went back down to the street, grabbed my bags and took them up, then carried my bike up the two flights of stairs and shut the door. I was tired, smelly and hungry (you'll see those three words repeated quite a lot in this book!), so I stripped off my cycling kit and hopped in to the shower.

Here begins the evening routine of the long-distance cyclist. I threw my cycling shorts, socks and top in to the bottom of the shower and as I showered, I did a little dance on them all. I accept that this is hardly a AAA rated washing routine, but given the circumstances it's the best I could do. Once I am washed and my clothes are also rinsed, I give them a squeeze, wrap them in a towel and give them a further squeeze to remove the majority of the water. Then I find (hopefully) some hangers out of the wardrobe and hang everything up to drip-dry. As everything is Lycra (yes, I am a MAMMIL, a Middle-Aged Man in Lycra), it doesn't take much drying and as long as it's not too cold usually everything is almost dry by the morning. If it isn't dry (socks are the worst culprit), it can go under a bungee cord on my rack to flutter in the breeze until it is.

Now showered and less smelly, I donned my shorts and Amicii tee shirt and went downstairs to look for something to eat. I found the same lady again and asked if there was a restaurant.

"Yes, but it's closed".

OK. "Does the room include breakfast?", I asked.

"No, but you can pay extra for breakfast", she replied.

"What time is breakfast?", I asked.

"8.30 to 9.30", she said.

I wanted to be long-gone by then, so it looked as if breakfast would be taken on the road.

I referred to Google again for somewhere to eat and it seemed like "Pizza Deja Vu" was the best option. I walked out in to the night and in to the square, up some steps and over the Aiud River. This did seem like quite a pretty little town – sorry, city. The Liceul Tehnologic Aiud (Aiud Technical College) was a very pretty building, as was the "Sfinții Trei Ierarhi" cathedral and the "Cetatea Aiud" (Aiud Citadel). If I had more time, I would have definitely like to have stayed a few hours more the following day. After walking over to "Pizza Deja Vu", I was a bit disappointed to find that it was closed, despite Google saying otherwise. I found myself back in the square outside Hotel Magnolia again and this time I opted for "Restaurant Capitol", five minutes walk away. This was most definitely open and after a few minutes I found myself tucking in to a delicious pizza and a beer.

With my hunger sated, I headed off back to the hotel to rest. It wasn't late, but I was truly tired. My final action of the evening was a quick video call with Jill and I was done for the day.

*Aiud Cathedral*

# Day 2 – Aiud to Lipova

144 miles

This needed to be a big day. I was trying to get back on schedule and by the end of the day I ought to be in Arad. I was awake early anyway and without the prospect of breakfast to look forward to I concentrated on getting away as soon as possible. I dressed and packed everything away quickly, then struggled down the marble staircase with my panniers and my bike.

I pressed "start" on my GPS at 6.42am and wobbled off up the road. It was somewhat colder at 11°C than the 27° of yesterday, but I expected it to warm up later. It was also quite foggy, so I turned on my lights and I was wearing just about all my cycling tops, with my day-glo yellow shirt on top to ensure I was seen by traffic.

Once again I abandoned my original planned route and stuck to the E81, hoping to make faster progress and make up time. I was hoping that even though today was Monday, the majority of the traffic would still be on the motorway. A couple of miles out of Aiud, I passed a Lukoil petrol station and thought about stopping to see if there was anything that might pass for breakfast, but although it did claim to have coffee and a mini-market, it looked pretty closed. Never mind, I was sure something else would turn up.

A little further on, I passed a building site of what looked like a hotel, but on closer inspection it seemed like it had been abandoned. There was a sign outside saying "De Vanzare" (for sale) and a couple of telephone numbers. I imagine that this had been somebody's grand business plan, but since the opening of that section of the A10 motorway in November 2021, the passing trade had declined almost to zero and the project was aborted.

The road here was fairly flat, tracking along the floodplain of the Mureș, with arable land to my left and rolling hills to my right. I passed a number of businesses selling shiny new agricultural implements as well as private residences, often single-storey buildings with red-tiled roofs. As I rode past these properties, I often heard and sometimes saw dogs barking. As long as they stayed behind the fences I didn't worry.

I passed through the town of Teiuș, which had a couple of supermarkets, but it was still early and they weren't open. All of the towns I passed through in Romania seemed to have beautifully ornate churches, or "Biserica", in the Gothic or "Brancoveanu" style. I'm no expert in such matters, but Wikipedia suggests that "Romania is one of the most religious of European countries and the majority of the country's citizens are Orthodox Christians."

By 8.15am I was approaching the city of Alba Iulia, administrative centre of Alba County. Traffic was building now, as to be expected. I left the E81 and took the DN1 towards the centre. I was mostly navigating via Google Maps at this point, so I kept having to stop and check which way I would turn at junctions. The DN1 was a dual carriageway and didn't have a shoulder either, so I wasn't particularly comfortable with the increasing amount of traffic. I needn't have worried though, as just after the start of the road, I saw a cycle path on the right. I wasn't expecting this, but it was very welcome, especially as it was the other side of the Armco barrier, safe from the traffic. This continued for a couple of miles, but then I ran in to a stretch of major roadworks. The cycle path disappeared, as did the pavement and one side of the road, pushing all the traffic on to the other side. I didn't fancy dicing with that traffic, so I continued on through the roadworks, bumping along the gravel and weaving in and out of the construction traffic. The road workers didn't seem to mind, in fact they often pulled to one side to let me through, which was very much appreciated. I emerged at the other end of the roadworks, much to the amusement of the pupils of the Dorin Pavel Technical College (Liceul Tehnic Dorin Pavel) as I weaved between them.

I consulted Google Maps again and figured out that I could now perhaps re-join my planned route, given that the E81 was becoming too busy to safely ride on, so I loaded the route in to my GPS.

"Do you want to navigate to the start?", it asked.

Bearing in mind that the start of this route was in Viișoara, I replied no. I continued down the "Strada Ardealului" and as I crossed the "Piaţa Alessandria" it beeped at me:

"Course found!"

The GPS then guided me along the cobbled "Strada Mihai Viteazul" and through the "Poarta I a Cetăţii" (The 1st Gate of the Fortress) and up a steep cobbled hill to the 2$^{nd}$ gate of the Fortress. Through the 2$^{nd}$ gate and I was now on to a beautiful plaza outside the 3$^{rd}$ gate.

I had read about Alba Iulia while I was planning my route and knew that it was a historically important centre since Roman times, at one time becoming the capital of Transylvania and some of its neighbouring territories. The Alba Carolina Citadel itself was constructed during the Habsburg rule in Transylvania from 1715 and is a star-shaped fortress sitting atop a hill. Inside the fortress walls sit a number of impressive buildings, developed by Charles VI, Holy Roman Emperor. Inside the fortress are The Union Hall, The National History Museum of Unification, the Princely Palace (Voivodal Palace), the Orthodox cathedral, the Roman Catholic cathedral, the

Batthyaneum Library, the Roman Catholic bishop's palace, the Apor Palace, and the University of Alba Iulia.

I stopped a few times to take some quick photographs as I passed through the old town, yet again wishing I had more time to explore. This was definitely a place I would love to revisit. I then passed on to the central park, a small, but very pretty park containing a number of attractions, including the Union Monument, celebrating the union of Transylvania with Romania in 1918; the Kinetic Fountain as well as other statues. In the background I there was also some soothing piped music, which just helped to set the scene.

*Alba Iulia*

I ended up doing a couple of laps of the park, not intentionally, but my GPS kept beeping at me, telling me first to turn this way, then that way, constantly telling me I was off-course. I eventually figured out which way it wanted me to go and headed off to the west. Just as I left the square, I spotted an inviting-looking shop to my right – "Dragon Pan", a bakery – it was nearly 9am and this looked like an ideal spot for breakfast.

"Breakfast" consisted of a bottle of Coke, a cup of coffee and a couple of pastries. I didn't really know what was in them as I couldn't understand the descriptions. As it turned out, one was apple and the other cherry (I think) and they were both delicious.

I rode out of the city, now following my planned route, down the DJ107A. DJ is short for "drum judeţean", regional road, so I was surprised to find that even this road had a fully-segregated cycle path. This did eventually run out, but not until a couple of miles out of town. I was back out in to the countryside now, still with the river Mureș to my left and hillside to my right. The sun was out, the temperature had risen to the high teens/low twenties, the road was quiet, with a great surface – what more could you want?

I rode through some pretty little villages, with well-kept houses – this must be the "wealthy" commuter belt for Alba Iulia. The villages gradually gave way to farms and open countryside, with maize appearing to be the favoured crop. Every now and then I'd pass fields with old-fashioned haystacks, something that you just don't see in the UK any more, in these days of plastic-wrapped round bales. There were also plenty of fruit trees; I didn't stop to make sure, but I think I saw damsons, figs and apricots. People were also out gathering sweet chestnuts from the trees that lined the road.

After 45 miles I rolled in to the town of Geoagiu. I knew there was a supermarket here, but as my schedule was still out of sync, I opted to stop at a petrol station instead. I grabbed a bottle of drink and an ice-cream and sat on the kerb and ate and drank. As I sat there, a group of Roma children came up to me with outstretched hands asking for money. Unfortunately they were out of luck, as I didn't have any coins and I wasn't going to hand them any of the few notes I had. Up until now, I'd bought everything with Google Pay, although I had brought a small amount of cash with me. In Romania I found that everywhere seemed to have contactless payment facilities – even in some of the remote areas I passed through.

From Geoagiu towards Simeria, a lot of the road had been recently resurfaced and was beautifully smooth. Just before I crossed the river to the south, there was a prominent hill, which turns out to be the Uroi Hill and is a site of significant archaeological discoveries dating back to the Iron Age. I passed quickly through Simeria heading now for Deva. This was supposed to be the destination for day one, as it was about 100 miles from Viișoara. I'd done a pretty good job of catching up, as it was just gone noon as I arrived. The road in to Deva was a little busy, but most of it had a small shoulder, so it wasn't too bad, apart from the final junction, where I had to cross both lanes of traffic to take the road in to the centre.

Deva seemed like a very modern town, with plenty of shops and high-rise apartments lining the broad avenues. Overlooking the city though, is the Fortress of Deva, sitting at the top of a (presumably extinct?) volcano, dating from the 13$^{th}$ century. It is possible to ride to the top in a funicular railway. Perhaps another day – another one to add to the list. As I left Deva, I popped in to a petrol station to buy something for lunch. There wasn't a lot of choice, but I settled on a packet of Tuc biscuits and some salami sticks – and an ice-cream, or course!

The first part of the road outside Deva was a bit scary – yet again it was the section between the town and the first motorway junction and it was a couple of miles of dual carriageway with plenty of lorries and no shoulder. Also, as the slip road to the motorway approached, the road turned uphill, so I wasn't exactly speeding along. When I arrived at the slip road, rather than trying to look over my shoulder for a gap in the traffic, I stopped and waited until there was a gap and ran across instead. Once I was past this hurdle, I found out that the traffic for Deva was actually joining the road at the same junction, driving up the hill and performing a u-turn at the top to take them back down in to the city. I was now on a three-lane highway competing with lorries, on a bicycle! It was only a few hundred metres, but that was enough for me.

A few miles outside Deva lies Mintia-Deva power station, which you can't help but notice because it is truly gargantuan. This was Romania's third largest power plant before it was recently decommissioned. It was coal-fired, burning 110 million metric tonnes of coal in its lifetime.

I'd loaded my second day's route in to my GPS now, which was Deva to Arad, another roughly 100 mile chunk. While planning this section, I'd pretty much followed the cycle route shown on the map and this stayed south of the river. A few miles after Mintia, my route left the DN7 at Săcămaș and followed the DN68A along the southern edge of the valley. As I went further along this road, the towns and villages became smaller and further apart. Then, just after I passed over the motorway heading to Timișoara further south, the tarmac stopped. I was now on a concrete road, but it had obviously seen better days. My teeth jarred as I bumped from section to section, then, just the other side of Tisa, even the concrete ran out and I was on a gravel track. Ironically, to the right of me I could see a massive infrastructure project underway, which I believe to be a major railway upgrade. At times it was hard to determine which way

I should go as in places the road had been bulldozed to make way for the new railway line. Added to this, there were quite a few lorries carrying stone from a nearby quarry to use in construction. Not wanting to tangle with these, I pulled off the track as soon as I saw or heard them coming.

Eventually, some 20 miles down the road near the town of Căprioara the tarmac reappeared. From here I'd plotted a detour off to Săvârșin, not for any other reason than I'd spotted a "Rompetrol" station on the map and it was time to refuel!

I crossed the Mureș again via the steel bridge, erected in 1906 and recently restored. The steel bridge replaced the original wooden one built in 1872 to carry salt from Valea Mare. Unfortunately this bridge "collapsed under the weight of carts overloaded with salt and pulled by several pairs of oxen".

Now the Săvârșin Rompetrol was a cut above the other petrol stations I'd visited – they had a good range of drinks, including Aqua Carpatica and paninis, which could even be heated up – the luxury! And ice-cream.

I did consider that I might stay on the main road at Săvârșin and just head straight for Arad, but the brief section I rode to the Rompetrol station and back made me change my mind. It was the main road to

Arad, as the motorway looped to the south via Timișoara. I headed back over the bridge to Valea Mare and continued on the back road. It wasn't too bad a road now and although the surface could have been better, it was still tarmac.

It was hot though. I'd been cycling for over nine hours and the temperature was in the high twenties, touching 30°C at times. I passed through a number of small villages then the tarmac ran out again just the other side of Bata. In retrospect I should have probably stayed on the DJ682, but the cycle route followed the river more closely. Then I ran in to the railway construction zone again – more gravel, more lorries and at one point I went half a mile or so up the railway, instead of staying on the road. I retraced my steps and scrambled down an embankment back on the road again. Surely it couldn't get any worse?

Yes, it could. Just the other side of Lalașint the road ran out completely! I rode in to a wooded area and the "road" became more akin to a forestry track. To cap it all off, there were even some people there cutting up wood with chainsaws. I'm not entirely sure what they thought as I bumped past them through the puddles on my bike, but it was probably not complementary.

The "forestry track" didn't last long though and the road reappeared at Belotinț. I'd been on the road for 12 hours now and although there was still plenty of daylight, I was getting a little weary. The nearest towns of Chelmac and Ususău didn't hold much promise of accommodation though. The best option looked like Lipova and that was still 15 miles away. Oh well, at least it was cooler now. I stopped at a mini-market in Ususău for one last drink. I needed a sugar boost to get me the last few miles. Half an hour later I was at the outskirts of Lipova. I pulled up and got my phone out to look for somewhere to stay. Here I followed a routine – open app; search for accommodation; sort by price, lowest to highest; pick accommodation with lowest price. On this occasion this appeared to be "Pensiunea Oxana", not in Lipova (there didn't appear to be any accommodation in Lipova!), but in Radna, on the other side of the river. I opened Google Maps and set it as a destination. It wasn't far, but Google decided to take me over an old metal bridge, which looked as if it might have been fenced off at some time, but said fence had long been broken down. Still, there was a young couple walking over it, so it must be OK. Shortly later I was outside the door of  Pensiunea Oxana, only it was very much closed. Back to the app. The nearest hotel and indeed the only other available in Lipova, was "Casa Maria Magdalena", just down the road. This also claimed to have "Restaurant Maria Magdalena" on the same premises, so looked like a good bet.

Back down the road again to Casa Maria Magdalena, which was easy enough to find, but not so easy to get in to. What appeared to be the front door was closed, but there was a sign with an arrow pointing to the side. I followed the arrow and arrived at a metal gate, which I pushed open and went inside. It was all very quiet, but there were a couple of men smoking outside.

"Hotel?", I asked, to which they gestured to some steps. I left my bike and went up the steps in to a dining room, which was also deserted.

"Hello…", I called. No reply. I walked towards the kitchen. "Hello…", I called a little louder.

"Hello", came a distant reply. Shortly afterwards a lady arrived, who fortunately spoke perfect English. I'd soon arranged a room for the night, which included breakfast at a more breakfast-ish time. I was shown to my room which was a distinct improvement over last night's hotel. I left my bike in the courtyard under a gazebo, carried my bags up to my room and began my usual routine – shower, while dancing on my clothes, hang clothes up to dry and get changed in to shorts and Amicii tee shirt. I sat down in my room and made a quick progress update video for Facebook before heading back downstairs.

The lady had vanished by the time I went downstairs again, so I was unable to ask her about restaurant Maria Magdalena. I went outside and around to the other side of the building to where the "Restaurant Maria Magdalena" sign was. I walked through the gate, but again it looked pretty closed. There were three men, who appeared to be unblocking a drain outside, who confirmed my suspicions. Dinner now looked like a distant hope.

Somewhat disappointed, I walked up the road towards a petrol station I'd spotted earlier. I didn't particularly want to dine "a la petrol station", but all the restaurants seemed to be in Lipova, on the other side of the river, about 20 minutes walk away. I guess I could have unlocked my bike and cycled over, but I'd done enough cycling for the day, thanks. Just then, I noticed a shop across the road that was still open. It didn't look much, but it was worth a look. I bought some cake and some drink as there wasn't much else on offer. Back across the road to the hotel again I retired to my room for a snack-fest before a quick video call with Jill and turning in for the night.

Day two had been a challenging day due to the route I'd selected. Still, I'd ridden 144 miles and was only 20 miles short of my "day two" target, so I was satisfied with that.

*Deva Citadel*

# Day 3 – Lipova to Szeged

94 miles

I was awake early, which seemed to become a pattern on this trip. I usually collapsed exhausted in to my bed early, as can be imagined, awaking early as a result. I dressed and packed as much as I could in to my panniers and headed downstairs to look for some breakfast at 8am. I wasn't disappointed this morning, as I was presented with a plate full of delicious-looking food. There was a toasted ham and cheese sandwich, some tortillas with ham and egg, bread, jam, soft cheese and slices of ham, mortadella and salami. All washed down with a glass of juice and a coffee. It was a welcome change to eat actual "food", rather than petrol station offerings. Needless to say, there was nothing left but crumbs.

I returned to my room to prepare for the day's riding. I removed my Amicii tee shirt and shorts and carefully rolled them up and stored them in my bags. My clothes from last night were still a bit damp, so I grabbed another pair of shorts, shirt and socks. I applied a generous dollop of chamois cream to the pad and I was ready.

Some explanation may be required here, for those that aren't familiar with cycling... Cycling shorts have a pad in them, that traditionally was made of chamois leather, but nowadays is made of cushioning foam of varying densities, with a top surface that helps to wick moisture and provide a soft feel against your skin. You don't wear any underwear with cycling shorts, as this would wrinkle up and cause chafing and saddle sores. Instead, you use a "chamois cream" that is usually based on mineral oil and includes lanolin and aloe to prevent chafing and sores. In my LEJOG in 2014, I had ridden in the pouring rain from Taunton to Kidderminster, 140 miles in total and at the end of that ride, I had a huge saddle-sore. I cleaned it with surgical spirit (ouch!), but to no avail – in the following days it became an open sore about the size of a 50 pence piece. I completed LEJOG, but not without the help of analgesic cream and an extra pair of shorts. Consequently, I was keen to avoid a repetition of this on "Stella's Journey". My evening routine, as well as a shower, included application of surgical spirit to my bottom, in an attempt to prevent saddle-sores in the first place.

I grabbed everything and went downstairs and out in to the courtyard. It was pouring down with rain. It wasn't cold, about 16°C, but I wasn't relishing the thought of a wet day in the saddle. I sat under the gazebo and pulled on my neoprene overshoes, which would help keep my feet a little warmer. There's no "magic bullet" to cycling in the rain. If you ride for long enough, you are going to get wet, no matter what you wear. I had eschewed my lightweight jacket for this trip in favour of a traditional cycling cape. There are advantages and disadvantages with these – the main advantages are that, because they are large, they cover your entire body, eliminating the need for waterproof leggings and because they are open at the bottom, there's plenty of ventilation, helping to avoid the build up of perspiration. The main disadvantage is that because they are large, they tend to billow in the wind and this can occasionally lead to unintentional, involuntary changes in direction. Another disadvantage I might add, it that they sometimes prevent you from seeing your GPS!

Suitably "togged up", I pushed my bike out of the courtyard and headed back over the bridge to the south side of the river again. Destination: Arad.

For some reason or other, my GPS had other ideas and on the other side of the bridge I ended up heading east again instead of west. Then we went through the usual routine of beeps and bleeps and "off course", "make a u-turn" and "course found" messages until it decided I should ride up a street that was closed for resurfacing. Never one to argue, I skilfully swerved around the barriers and complied with instructions. The road was only "closed" for half a mile or so and a few minutes later I was westbound on the DJ682 heading to Neudorf, Zăbrani and Arad.

Considering this was only a "DJ" road, there was a surprising amount of lorries. I later found out that this appears to be a short cut or "rat run" through to

Timișoara, but luckily all the lorries turned off after Neudorf. I was still following the river Mureș, but the valley had opened out significantly and the river was now three or four miles north of me. The terrain was flat and I was riding past fields of maize and sunflowers. I rode straight through Neudorf, but in Zăbrani my GPS insisted I zig-zag through the back streets. I obviously hadn't "fixed" this part of the route before I left the UK. I ignored the part that sent me up what looked like somebody's driveway though.

After riding for just one hour, the rain stopped, so I pulled in to a convenient bus stop and removed my cape in the town of Aluniș. The sun soon came out and the temperature started to climb. Another hour further on and I was in the outskirts of Arad, making good progress. Arad was the end of my "day 2" route, so just after I crossed the Traian Bridge – a steel Cantilever truss bridge, built in 1913 (at the end of the Second World War, the bridge was dynamited, but the structure was not severely damaged) – my GPS did it's little tune to mark "course complete". I stopped in a park by the river and loaded "3 – Arad to Kecskemet" (131 miles). I'm not sure how I'd managed to sneak in a 131 mile section, but it didn't matter, as I'd already arranged to stay that night with a bewelcome.org host, Peter, in Szeged, Hungary.

Arad, in western Romania, is a large city with a population of nearly 150,000 and I'd routed my ride around it, rather than through it. I'm not a city-dweller, although I did briefly live in London and also in Santiago, Chile, for several years, but I much prefer smaller towns. It looked very much to be a busy industrial city and while I'm sure there may be plenty of historical buildings, my route seems to have avoided all of them! Initially I followed a cycle path along the north bank of the Mureș and I was surprised with how excellent the cycling infrastructure was, when I came upon a hastily erected fence and a huge section missing. A new bridge over the river was under construction and the cycle route had been a temporary victim of progress. I back-tracked a couple of hundred yards and ad-libbed my way past the works and back to my route.

Shortly after my impromptu detour, I spotted a Lidl supermarket. It was 11.30am and I thought that elevenses might be in order. I crossed the dual-carriageway, locked my bike and went in to see what was on offer. A few minutes later I emerged with pan au chocolat, bananas, iced coffee and a bottle of Aqua Carpatica and sat on the floor munching away. I refilled my bidons with the water and strapped the bottle with the remaining water on my rack for later. It was warming up and I was pretty sure I'd need it.

Back on to the dual-carriageway (well, on to the cycle path beside it) I continued to the busy roundabout junction with "Calea Aurel Vlaicu". This looked fairly imposing at first glance, with lots of traffic, but yet again all I had to do was stick to the cycle-path and I was safely across and heading west on the segregated bike path next to "Calea Aurel Vlaicu". Aurel, by the way,  was a Romanian engineer, inventor, aeroplane constructor and early pilot…

The bike path continued all the way to the outskirts of Arad, some 3 miles later, passing apartment blocks, shopping malls and then factories. This was the main DN7 road and was very busy, especially with lorries, but once I'd passed the junction for the motorway it got a little quieter. I opted to stay on the DN7 all the way to the Hungarian border, mainly because there weren't many other options, or those that there were, would have taken me out of my way. Despite the fact there was a motorway running parallel to the road, there were still an awful lot of lorries and this part of the road wasn't at all enjoyable.

This part of Romania (and the vast majority of Hungary all the way to Budapest) is pan-flat and seems to be dedicated almost entirely to the production of maize. Romania produces 17% of corn in the EU, second only to France at 21% (Hungary is joint 3rd place with Italy at 9%), according to the US department of agriculture. By the way, "corn" and "maize" are one and the same thing – in the USA it is almost always referred to as "corn", but in the UK maize refers to the crop grown in fields whereas corn refers to the harvested product. The flat terrain also meant that I felt the full force of the wind that was blowing. It wasn't a very strong wind, but it made itself felt. Given that the temperature was now over 30°C, the rest of the day felt like riding in to a large hairdryer set to "warm".

Ten miles out of Arad approaching another motorway junction I'd had enough of the lorries and spotted temporary relief in the form of a transport cafe on the other side of the road, so I made a hasty u-turn and cut across the central reservation. Just as I rolled up, so did a coach that began disgorging passengers. Not wanting to be at the back of the queue for lunch I walked briskly inside and stood at the counter. I chose a vegetable tortilla and salad and grabbed a couple of bottles of fizzy drink, then went and sat by the window to await the arrival of my food. When it arrived, it was quite a large portion, but under normal circumstances it wouldn't have presented much of a problem. However, after eating half of it I was struggling to eat any more. I don't know if it was the heat, but I just couldn't face it.

Back out on the road, I set off through Pecica and diverted off the main road just for a short while to give me some respite from the lorries. Back on again towards Nădlac, 15 miles away and close to the border with Hungary. Yet more monotonous flat road, fields of maize, lorries and warm hairdryers. I stopped for a drink and a brief rest about half way at a lay-by, where there was nothing but a picnic table and a dilapidated dumpster.

Continuing further I ran in to a queue of lorries outside Nădlac, all pulled over to the side of the road. Cars were overtaking this queue, so I followed suit. This was a tricky manoeuvre, at this was a single-carriageway road and both cars and I frequently had to make a dive as close as we could to the right hand lane to allow cars and lorries travelling in the opposite direction to pass. I fully expected this situation to continue all the way to the border, but after a couple of miles, the queue ended at a control with a couple of policemen who had stopped the lorries. Through the town, out the other side and not long after I arrived at the border.

"First time in Romania?", asked the border control officer, as he stamped my passport.

"Yes", I replied. And with that, I left the country.

*Border crossing, Romania/Hungary*

# CHAPTER 8. HUNGARY

I rode a couple of hundred metres and arrived at Hungarian passport control. The interaction was similarly brief.

"Welcome to Hungary", I was greeted.

"Thanks", I replied. And that was it.

I was now in the Schengen area, inside of which border controls no longer exist. Romania, whilst still in the EU, is not inside the Schengen area, hence the controls.

I paused at the "Welcome to Hungary" sign for a photo and uploaded it to Facebook with the message "that's a milestone", which for me at least, it was. It was now half-past one (again), as entering Hungary the clocks had gone back an hour from  Eastern European Time (EET; UTC+02:00) to Central European Time (CET; UTC+01:00). Almost instantly the trucks on the main road disappeared, preferring to head on to the motorway rather than staying on route 43. That was fine by me. Once again, it looks like "43" had at one time been the main road, but since the opening of the M43 in 2015 it had been relegated to the "old road" status. I had planned on taking the 43 to Makó, then following a cycle-route to Kecskemét.

However, as my destination for the day was now Szeged, I would have to ad-lib it from Makó.

The next ten miles or so passed uneventfully, once more past fields and fields of maize, but without the lorries now. Often a separate cycle path appeared next to the roadside too, sometimes on the left, sometimes on the right. Generally I found the surface on the cycle path to be better than the surface of the road, so although I felt perfectly safe on the road, I opted to ride on the cycle path instead. These cycle paths also went on for miles, so there was no disadvantages to using them at all.

I arrived at the first turning for Makó, cancelled my GPS route and headed in to town, yet again on the cycle path. I was beginning to really like Hungary! Then, on the left appeared a familiar sign – Tesco! I thought now might be a good time to top up on food and water, as it was 4pm (or 5pm Romanian time). I also managed to purchase some sun cream, as I hadn't brought any with me and was a little bit sunburnt. OK, I was a lot sunburnt. The lady at the pharmacy offered me some Flamazine burn cream, which I rejected. As long as it didn't get any worse, I could cope. At least I could honestly tell Jill that I'd taken precautions now, as she had been chastising me for not using sun cream thus far.

I continued through town and out the other side, once more crossing the river Mureș, that had been my constant companion since day one. It didn't have far to go though – the Mureș joins the river Tisa at Szeged, which in turn flow south and joins the Danube near Belgrade. My next destination was indeed Szeged, my stop for the night. I had been communicating via WhatsApp with Peter, my host for the night, who informed me he'd be at home around 7pm. I had plenty of time, so I didn't push too hard to arrive. I continued on the 43, which would take me all the way in to town. I didn't really know how far away that was though, as curiously, Hungarian roads don't appear to have distance signs at all. There were small green signs with numbers on them, which I guessed were probably km signs, but I didn't know whether that was the distance to Szeged, or the distance from Makó.

In time I arrived at the outskirts of the city, so I fired up Google maps and punched in Peter's address. It was a bit tricky navigating, as I didn't have anything to hold my phone on my bike, so I turned up the volume and threw my phone in my handlebar bag and listened for the voice prompts instead. It wasn't a brilliant system, but it worked well enough.

Szeged is a fairly large city – the third largest in Hungary, with a population of over 160,000 – and as I navigated through it what must have been the evening rush hour it left me with a good impression. I crossed the river Tisa at the Belvárosi Bridge, an impressive steel bridge designed by Gustave Eiffel (yes, that Eiffel) and Feketeházy János and finished in 1883. It was destroyed by the Germans in 1944 and reconstructed after the war in 1948. The architecture of the city is most impressive, but it may come as a surprise to discover that the vast majority of the buildings were destroyed in a flood in 1879: 95% of the buildings in the centre were destroyed. After the flood, Emperor Franz Joseph visited the town and declared that the city would be rebuilt, even more beautiful than before, hence the grandiose buildings and boulevards that grace the centre. The boulevards have also given the modern-day planners an opportunity to provide for all road users as well and yet again I was very impressed with the bike paths. In fact, I followed these all the way to Peter's apartment.

I arrived early, with almost an hour to spare, so I let Peter know and headed back out again to look for a beer. I found a small bar not far away and sat down with the locals to pass the time. My Hungarian is non-existent and they didn't speak any English so the conversation didn't flow very much, but there were plenty of hand-signals and I very much enjoyed the beer.

Not long after, Peter messaged that he'd arrived home, so I rode back to his apartment block, where he met me outside. We left my bike in the entrance lobby with all the rest (cycling is the preferred transport in Szeged) and went up to his flat. He invited me to use the shower; I must have smelt pretty bad and even offered to wash my cycling kit (properly, in a washing machine), which I quickly accepted. After a quick shower, I invited Peter out to dinner at a local restaurant of his choice. He chose well and we sat outside on the terrace of an Italian restaurant, discussing our shared love of travel. It transpires that in 2024 Peter plans to take some months out to travel around the Mediterranean, so if you can put him up for the night, let me know and I'll put you in touch! Half way through the evening I had my regular video call from Jill, who was a little concerned about me staying with a complete stranger, so I introduced her to Peter and he confirmed he wasn't a mass-murderer, so we were all good. After dinner we strolled back to Peter's flat and the evening was over. We both had an early start in the morning, so I crashed out on the sofa with Peter's cat for company (don't tell Stella!).

## DAY 4 – SZEGED TO BUDAPEST

118 miles

In the morning we were both up early. Peter because he had to go to work and me, because I was on a mission. We had a quick breakfast of bread, cheese and ham, with a cup of coffee, then it was down to the lobby with all my kit and off I rode. I'd discussed the possibility of cycling north from Szeged on route 5, once again the "old road". He thought it would be OK, because he also imagined that the majority of the traffic would be on the motorway, which ran almost parallel. Route 5 ran all the way to Budapest, but the first stage was to get to Kecskemét, about half way. I was soon out of town, having safely navigated the bike paths and on to route 5. As we had thought, it wasn't too busy, so it looked like I should be able to make good progress. The terrain was still flat - I was crossing the Great Hungarian Plain, as I had since yesterday. The plain occupies more than half of the territory of modern Hungary. Today didn't seem to be so windy either, but I imagined that it might increase as the day got warmer. The temperature was already in the twenties though, but as luck would have it the first section of the route was tree-lined, which offered some welcome shade. I alternated between riding on the road and riding on the bike paths, the latter being very good, but some sections had been affected by tree roots, which made it bumpy at times.

After a couple of hours I arrived in Balástya, not a very large town, but I did spot what looked like a mini-market, so I thought it might be a good place for a pause. I left my bike up against the railings outside and popped in to see what was available. This time I managed to pick up a few bits and pieces, including a couple of bananas and some pastries, as well as the usual bottles of water and fizzy drink. Regarding the latter, I always went for the full-sugar version – I most definitely wasn't on a diet!

I spotted a bus shelter on the other side of the road and thought it would make a good place to sit for a few minutes and make one of my regular video updates. Then, I was back on the road again, heading north. A little further on, I stopped on a bike path and thought I'd try my hand at something a little more "artistic" than just sitting and chatting to my phone. I pulled out my selfie-stick, which I had tried to use once and found it was pretty useless, but it doubled as a tripod. I set it on the ground and set it recording. I then rode back a bit on the bike path, rode past the tripod, doubled back, turned the phone around, rode past it again, then doubled back and stopped the recording. The intention was to make a movie of me cycling past and off in to the distance, but when I started trying to edit the clip I had recorded, my phone went in to "video editor needs to update" mode, so somewhat frustrated, I abandoned the plan. Guess I should have tested it out before I left.

On and on I rode, past the patchwork of fields, past derelict petrol stations and restaurants – victims of the new motorway – counting down the km markers to Budapest. Another couple of hours passed and I rolled in to Kiskunfélegyháza (I read the sign, but I didn't try and pronounce it), a little larger than

Balástya, but still no buzzing metropolis. I saw a fast-food cabin alongside the road, although I didn't see what kind of fast-food it was serving. I pulled over to take a look, thinking at least I could buy a drink or something. Inside were two ladies cooking and serving up lángos, a deep-fried flatbread. Looking at the pictures on the side of the cabin I initially thought they were pizza, bringing back dark memories of once having a deep-fried pizza in batter in Spalding, Lincolnshire. Various flavours were available, as I could see with the aid of my translation app, but I eventually settled on a sweet variety, with jam and sugar. Now, I am known to have a sweet tooth, but this was absolutely delicious. Plenty of sugar and carbohydrates to keep me going for a few hours.

Another 20 miles further on and I arrived at Kecskemét, which was a much larger city. As I arrived at the outskirts, I saw numerous signs for Mercedes-Benz, the city's largest employer. Shortly later I rode past a huge factory, topped with a huge, rotating, three-pointed star. I was still following route 5, although now I was almost exclusively riding alongside it on the bike path. Route 5 itself had become a lot busier and was often a dual carriageway, with signs prohibiting tractors, horse-drawn vehicles and bicycles. I diverted through the city centre to avoid the traffic, stopping for a few minutes in the central Liberty Square (Szabadság tér), enjoying the shade of the trees in the 30° heat.

My original route from Kecskemét was to have taken me on a loop to the west, joining up with the EuroVelo 6 "Atlantic to Black sea" route, which would then follow a tributary of the Danube all the way in to Budapest.  However, as I'd been making such good progress on route 5, I thought I'd stick with it and take advantage of the shorter distance. In retrospect, that was a bad move. Initially it wasn't too bad; there was still a bike path and where there wasn't, there was a pretty wide shoulder to ride on. The road was getting busier and busier though, with more and more lorries. At one point, while passing a junction, there were lorries passing me to my left and lorries merging on to route 5 from my right – this just wasn't fun any more. Then, without a warning, the sign appeared for no tractors, horse-drawn vehicles or bicycles, without any options as to where the aforementioned should go! It was too late for me, I was committed – I put my head down and carried on as fast as I could towards Lajosmizse, the next town. Then, as quickly as it had vanished, the bike path reappeared. This situation continued – Táborfalva, bike path, then after the town, no bike path, lots of lorries; Örkény – bike path; after Örkény, no bike path, even more lorries. Suddenly I was closely passed by a succession of articulated lorries. This was ridiculous, if I stayed on this road I was going to get killed, I had to do something. As soon as I could, I pulled off the main road and grabbed my phone. I could see that I was close to a turning for a town called Dabas. If I could get to that road, I could then take the back roads in to Budapest.

I waited for a gap in the traffic and rode as hard as I could for the turning for Dabas, breathing a huge sigh of relief as I got there. The difference was like chalk and cheese – one minute nose to tail lorries, the next, nothing, a quiet country lane. I even managed to make a short video as I rode along, letting everyone know what was happening. Then, just as I was uploading my video to our group chat, a black scruffy dog appeared from the bushes beside the road.

I stopped and he came towards me, nothing more than skin and bones. What to do? Well, the first thing I could do was to give him some of my biscuits. I still had plenty and could easily buy some more. He seemed very appreciative. I gave him some water from my bidon, making a pool in a nearby pothole for him to drink. As he lapped at the water, I messaged captain Ann. She quickly sent back a message with the Facebook pages of a couple of rescues close to me, one in Örkény, which I'd recently passed. I called the rescue in Örkény and spoke to a lady there, who seemed very concerned, but she couldn't help, because her van was in Budapest where they'd take another dog for an operation. She suggested another rescue, who might be able to help. I looked up that one and called them, but the number just rang out. I spent about an hour by the roadside, feeding my new friend biscuits and water, messaging and calling the local rescues to no avail. Eventually, a woman passed in a car and stopped to talk. I explained what was happening and she looked as if she might be about to help, but eventually she managed to convey her message, "This is a farm dog from nearby. I see him all the time..." Regrettably, there was nothing more I could do. I felt like a failure – if I'd have had my car, he would have been in the back already, but as it was, I had to leave him. If he was a farm dog, as the lady suggested, then they didn't deserve him.

I had to leave. It was half past three and I still had 40 miles to go until Budapest. With the weight of my new friend still on my mind, I continued down the road, until my GPS told me I had to turn right. I made the turn, found myself on a sandy track and promptly fell off. I wasn't going fast, so there was no damage, and I quickly composed myself and picked myself off the ground. A man in a truck had seen me fall and stopped to ask if I was OK. I assured him I was fine and we both went on our way.

I found another road to Dabas, then gradually zig-zagged my way north-east. I passed through a succession of villages without incident, then arrived at a "road closed" sign just outside Taksony. It looked as if there was some work being undertaken on the railway, rather than the road itself, but the diversion was down another sandy track, similar to the one that had recently caused my crash. I didn't relish the thought of another, so I gingerly made my way along the track, relieved to reach the end of the diversion without incident.

It was getting late now, about 6.30pm, but I was only just arriving at the outskirts of the city. I still had about 15 miles to go to get to the centre. I didn't have anywhere to stay in Budapest – I'd messaged a couple of BeWelcome hosts, but nobody had replied. Normally I would have looked at my phone at about this time and booked somewhere to stay, but I'd just about had enough of everything today – the trucks, the heat, falling off and not being able to help a stray dog. I made up my mind where I was going to stay; I was going to stay in the same hotel that Jill and I stayed at in July. I knew that I would soon be picking up the EuroVelo 6 and I knew that the EV6 ran right outside the hotel entrance. All I had to do was follow the cycle route.

That in itself was easier said than done. I did run in to the EV6 as I expected, but as previously explained, the EuroVelo routes are more of a concept than routes in reality. There are some signs, but not enough to rely on, so I was still very much using the navigation prompts of my GPS. After dicing with some trams, I crossed a large river, which I thought was the Danube, but was actually the Ráckevei-Duna river, a tributary. Shortly afterwards I did cross the Danube, on the modern Rákóczi Bridge, which fortunately has separate sections for trams, cars and bikes. At least now I was on the same side of the river as the hotel. From here, it was a straightforward ride on the bike path along the eastern side of the Danube until I got to the hotel. I remembered that the hotel was not long after the Széchenyi Chain Bridge, the most famous bridge in Budapest (actually designed by English engineer William Tierney Clark and built by Scottish engineer Adam Clark), but I kept riding past bridges and not finding the hotel, had I ridden past it? Soon I could see the Hungarian Parliament building on the other side of the river and I knew that was opposite the hotel; finally, there was the Chain Bridge and I was on familiar territory. I arrived at the hotel at 8.30pm. I'd ridden 118 miles in temperatures up to 34°C, it had taken me nearly 14 hours and I desperately hoped they had a room.

I pushed my bike through the door and across the marble flooring.

"Have you got a room please?", I asked.

The man at the reception tapped away on the computer behind his desk.

"I was here in July, with my wife", I added. The man asked for my name.

"Ah, yes", he said. "We have a room, but unfortunately not at the rate you had in July…"

I didn't care. My credit card would have to take the strain.

"I'm cycling from Romania to the United Kingdom for charity", I said, hoping this might help.

"Let me see what I can do", he replied.

Shortly afterwards, I was checked in to my room, overlooking the Danube and the Hungarian Parliament, with the best available rate, with a free breakfast included. I could have hugged him. But I didn't.

We parked my bike in the left-luggage room, I grabbed my panniers and headed up in the elevator for a much needed shower. I dumped everything on the floor in the room, did my shower routine on my clothes and rushed back downstairs to the restaurant where I managed to order something just before kitchen closed. Back to my room again and I just enough time for a Facebook post and video call with Jill before I was out like a light.

*Hungarian Parliament, Budapest*

# DAY 5 – BUDAPEST TO GYÖR

100 miles

I set my alarm in time for me to get up for breakfast at 7am, but I still woke up long before my alarm went off. I seemed to be waking up earlier and earlier each day. The breakfast was a buffet style "all you can eat" and I took advantage of that! After eating my fill, I returned to my room, collected my bags, my bike and I was ready to go at 7.37am.

I was looking forward to the next few days, as I would be following the EV6 up the river Danube and I was hoping that the route would be lorry-free. First things first though and I stood outside the hotel opposite the Hungarian Parliament building and made a quick video update for social media, before setting off northwards along the Danube.

The bike path ran alongside the "Slachta Margit rakpart" highway that skirts the Danube, that was busy with morning commuter traffic, but it was a segregated path, so it didn't present any problems. I criss-crossed other roads and tram lines at crossings and through underpasses and then the road took a detour through the Szentlélek tér (Holy Spirit Square), with some beautiful buildings and cobbled streets. It had rained overnight and the cobbles were a little slippery. I didn't want to risk falling off my bike again, as I'd noticed a pain on the right-hand side of my chest this morning, which I attributed to yesterday's fall. I passed Esernyős Szobrok (umbrella sculptures), which I thought was appropriate, given the rain. Back alongside the river I passed under Újpest Railway Bridge and continued along the bike path. Sometimes I rode past elegant riverside properties, sometimes there were cafes and restaurants, and sometimes I rode along the top of a dyke that ran alongside the river to prevent flooding, but almost always the bike path was well paved. Occasionally the EV6 looped away from the river and ran along route 11, but this wasn't a particularly busy road, linking together the towns and villages alongside the Danube. The road passed by the outskirts of many of the towns, which was a shame in a way, because it would have been nice to investigate further. This would have to be a trip for the future though, when I have more time in hand.

I passed Szentendre, Leányfalu and Tahitótfalu on the main road, before spotting a restaurant in Szentgyörgypuszta. More than a couple of hours had passed and I fancied a coffee. I had already ridden 25 miles, so it was now OK to stop, given my own self-imposed rules. The "rules" were that I should ride at least 25 miles (40km) before stopping for a break, then another 25 miles before stopping for lunch, etc. This broke the day up in to manageable chunks, or at least that was the idea. Sometimes it was too hot to ignore the need to quench my thirst and sometimes at my 25 mile intervals the opportunity didn't arise. If I thought that was going to me the case, I would buy something to eat and drink later.

I continued along route 11 and just after my stop the Danube widened out  - here it was nearly half a mile wide. I paused in Visegrád to take it all in and to grab a photograph. My GPS wanted to route me through the town centre, but on this occasion I ignored it, preferring to stay on the main road, or the bike path alongside, to admire the majestic views.

There was one view that I didn't like the look of though, that of the sky. There were some very dark looking clouds to the east and that meant only one thing. Surely enough, further down the road I felt the first droplets of rain. Luckily, a convenient bus shelter appeared in the nick of time and I took cover as the heavens opened. It was only a shower though and didn't last, so before long I was able to continue.

Route 11 then took a turn away from the river, cutting off one of the meanders, while the EV6 stuck close to the river. I might have been tempted to stay on the road and take the short cut, but I was so glad I didn't. The next three or four miles were just beautiful. There was a metalled bike path that ran right alongside the river, through the birch woods that lined it. At one point there was a slipway running down to the river and I just had to stop for a few squares of chocolate and a photograph. This was a world away from the problems of yesterday. I thought it almost couldn't get any better, but after only a few minutes it did, as I arrived at the city of Esztergom, with its Basilica sitting atop a rocky outcrop.

On the other side of the river now was Slovakia, linked to Esztergom via the Mária Valéria Bridge, over 500 metres in length. Interestingly, the metal bridge has been destroyed and rebuilt twice – once in 1919 and once in 1944. On the second occasion, differences between the Hungarian and Czechoslovakian governments meant that the bridge was never rebuilt until 2001!

After Esztergom the EV6 returned to the main road (the 11), which then joined with another main road that was much busier. There was still a good bike path though, so although it wasn't as pleasant, it was at least safe. The river wasn't far away, but it was out of sight now, the other side of fields and hedgerows, then behind rows of houses as I passed through the towns and villages. The route continued to follow the main road, but there were occasions where it did become a little confusing, as sometimes there were "no bicycles" signs, yet no apparent bike path. The locals seemed to ride along the pavement, so I followed suit. Conversely, at one section, the road and railway were squeezed between the hillside and the river, leaving no room for a shoulder or a bike path, so I was forced (and permitted) to ride along the main road for a few miles, once again mixing it with the lorries. Without a doubt, that part of the EV6 needs more work!

With just over 50 miles under my belt I stopped in Nyergesújfalu for lunch, which consisted of a pear, a peach and some water from the greengrocer just across the road from the Zoltek factory! I sat outside on a convenient picnic table and ate my lunch next to the dual carriageway.

Further along the road, the bike path was back and I had the familiar experience of riding alongside yet more fields of maize. I did wonder how they had managed to build the bike paths sometimes though. Often the roads were wide and they had just build them alongside, but I assumed that on occasions they had compulsorily purchased land from farms to build bike paths. A little further along the road (now route 10) I think I got my answer, as the bike path did a dog leg around a property through a field.

I turned on to route 1, which would take me all the way in to Györ. This road wasn't too busy, but it wasn't overly picturesque either, running as it did slightly inland from the river, through a series of industrial towns. I passed manufacturers of car parts, flexible hoses and biofuel, interspersed with more fields of maize. The last two may well be related, as the Internet tells me that "Maize is the predominant raw material (together with sugar cane) for the production of bioethanol, the most common and widespread biofuel, and at the same time the predominant raw material for biogas production, with the highest yields in Europe."

My next break from route 1 came at Komárom, 75 miles in, when I spotted an ice-cream kiosk. I probably should have had something more substantial than ice-cream at this point, but the temperature was back in to the 30's now and it hit the spot. While I was eating my ice-cream (double scoop tutti-frutti) I had a bit of an emotional wobble – when I have an ice-cream in the UK, Stella always gets the end of the cone and she sits patiently waiting for her little treat. Of course, there was no Stella with me and for some inexplicable reason that hit me quite hard.

After Komárom I was diverted off of route 1 for a while and rode through the suburbs and then, when the suburbs ended through a forest and across fields, all the time on a perfectly paved cycle path. It was obvious that this section of the EV6 had only recently been completed. Indeed, if you try and find it on Google maps, it's so recent that it doesn't exist! I reappeared back on route 1, or more correctly on a new cycle path right next to it and this situation, somewhat incredibly, continued all the way to Györ! This section, although I couldn't complain about the cycling infrastructure, was well and truly… Well… Boring.

Upon reaching the outskirts of the city, my GPS took me away from route 1 and through the back-streets, following EV6 all the way. I stopped just short of the centre, as I'd booked an Airbnb for the night and I needed to use Google to navigate me the last few hundreds of metres. A little while later I'd arrived, nine hours and 48 minutes after setting out. I followed the instructions in my email, grabbed the key from the key box and let myself in. I left my bike downstairs in the entrance hall, locked to a railing just in case, detached my bags and went up to the apartment, plonked myself in a chair and made a quick video for Facebook.

Shortly afterwards again I descended to the street, looking for somewhere to eat. I wasn't sure what I wanted, so I wandered the streets for a while looking for inspiration. That didn't arrive, however, so I'm sorry to say that eventually I ended up in MacDonalds. Quite how I failed to find something better I don't know.  Györ seemed to be quite a happening place, even on a Thursday night, but I guess I was just tired. Burger and fries duly consumed I went back to my Airbnb, made my customary video call with Jill and went to bed.

*Esztergom, Hungary*

# DAY 6 – GYÖR TO TULLN

109 miles.

I was awake at the crack of dawn again and made myself a coffee and a bowl of porridge for breakfast, before packing my bags and heading out! I realized I hadn't taken any photos of Györ at all the previous evening, so I grabbed a couple on the way out of town. Oddly enough, just down the road I passed a couple of guys singing blues songs. They were quite good and a bit of a crowd had gathered, but given it was just gone seven in the morning it seemed a bit strange to me.

I crossed the river Moson-Danube, which isn't a river in its own right, but is a branch of the Danube. I was about 5 miles inland of the Danube proper here and I wouldn't actually come near the Danube again for another 40 miles. Luckily, I wasn't on route 1 again though, as the EV6 continued along a more minor road parallel with it. Even though it was a minor road, it still had a good bike path, although some parts of it were again bumpy with tree roots.

I passed uneventfully through a number of towns and villages – Győrújfalu, Dunazeg, Ásványráró (which curiously has a flag similar to that of Scotland) before stopping in Halászi to buy some food for my "25 mile" snack. I needn't have worried to be honest, because that mark came at the town of Mosonmagyaróvár, which was much larger. Nevertheless, I stopped by the side of the road in a little park, sat at a handy picnic table and ate my food and made a video update. That done, I cut through the grounds of the university and the castle and was soon on my way out of the other side of town.

Yet more fields of maize passed (about 10 miles of them) until I arrived at the village of Rajka. Here, the EV6 left the road, passed through the pretty little village and headed in to the countryside. A mile or so later, I rode through some woods and appeared alongside the Moson-Danube again. Shortly afterwards, I turned right over a bridge, climbed a short hill on to a dyke, turned left and cycled past a barrier. Just past the barrier were a uniformed man and woman, who I assumed were Hungarian police, until I noticed the badges on their arms – it appeared that I was in Slovakia.

# CHAPTER 9. SLOVAKIA?

For some inexplicable reason I was surprised to find myself in Slovakia, as I didn't think my route went through it. I assumed that the south side of the Danube was in Hungary and the north side was Slovakia, so I was expecting to ride straight from Hungary in to Austria. As it is, there is a section of land south of the Danube, containing the towns of Petržalka, Jarovce, Rusovce and Čunovo which is part of Slovakia. As is often the case, this was not always so and indeed up until 1919 this section was part of Hungary and then the Austro-Hungarian Empire. After WW1, the Austro-Hungarian Empire was dissolved and the Czechoslovak state was established, but it's borders were not wholly defined. This part of Slovakia was annexed by Czechoslovak soldiers on the 1$^{st}$ of January 1919 and finally assigned to Czechoslovakia at the Paris Peace Conference. Anyway, brief history of this part of Slovakia completed. This is going to be a very short chapter, because I was only actually in Slovakia for 14.4 miles and just over an hour and a half.

I briefly chatted to the border guards on the dyke and then I went on my way. Yet again, although I knew I was cycling along the course of the River Danube, I couldn't actually see the river. I was either riding on top of a dyke, from which the Danube was hidden by trees, or on occasions I dropped off of the dyke and was riding on a road alongside the dyke. The dyke itself is very impressive and serves to protect that section of Slovakia from floods. These were constructed by the Government of Slovakia and largely financed by the EU Cohesion Fund and were completed in 2010.

The EV6 runs all the way along the dyke and seems very well used by cyclists, as well as for other sporting activities, like walking, running and roller blading. It also passes under a series of impressive bridges that cross from Bratislava to Petržalka. The last of these, while not particularly aesthetic, is the Lanfranconi Bridge, which interestingly has a separate deck for a cycle path.

After the Lanfranconi Bridge, the EV6 took a diversion away from the river, in the same direction as the highway, before heading east again on the top of a dyke towards the Austrian border.

Just before the border, on the right hand side of the dyke there was a bunker, "Bunker B-S 4", now designated as a museum. According to visitbratislava.com, "The bunker B-S 4 Lány is a remnant of the Bratislava Section of the Czechoslovak Fortification System from 1935-1938". Interestingly, it also says that "The original army bunker was entirely destroyed and has been reconstructed since 2011 by a group of volunteers whose work is based on the original documentation and photographs in order to put it back as it was in 1938."

It was now 11.30 and I'd ridden 50 miles, so it was time for a break. Fortuitously, right at that moment a transport cafe appeared, right on the border with Austria. I dumped my bike outside and walked through the entrance. You could instantly tell we were still in Slovakia, because the walls of the cafe were full of posters of ice hockey players clad in red, white and blue – ice hockey being Slovakia's number 1 sport.

I ordered a coffee, a pastry and an ice-cream (temperature was now in the high 20's) and went outside to eat. While I ate, a couple arrived with a Springer Spaniel, who ran up and down the grassy slope by the cafe and went to greet everyone who was sitting outside, including me. It was lovely to see him, running around so happily and it put a smile on my face! Elevenses consumed, I was back on the bike and literally 50 metres later, I was in Austria.

# Chapter 10. Austria

Well, I did say Slovakia was going to be a short chapter…

I was still riding along a dyke between the road and some fields to my right, once again containing maize. The Danube, or Donau, as it is known in Austria, was still a mile or so away to the north. The dyke gradually lowered in height and eventually I was riding alongside the road. I passed through the town of Wolfsthal towards Hainburg an der Donau, the imposing 11th century Heimenburg castle ruins towering over the town on a hill.

I left the main road, which by-passed the town and wound my way through the centre, past the old city walls and there in front of me, was the Danube. I rode along the side of the river for a mile or so before the route passed under the Andreas Maurer Bridge, then took a sharp turn to the left. I then wound my way back under the bridge and climbed a steep zig-zag path up to the bridge itself. The Danube here isn't so wide, but the bridge crosses the flood plain in its entirety, so is about 2km long. I crossed on the bike path, before doubling back on myself on to another dyke on the opposite side of the river.

*The blue Danube*

I was now riding along the north bank of the Danube, which passes through the Danube-Auen National Park. This is a huge area covering 93 square kilometres and is a natural floodplain for the Danube. The dyke I was riding along now stretched for 20 miles, all the way to Vienna. While I couldn't complain about the path, which was largely surfaced or gravelled, the sheer length of this stretch of the EV6 was mind-numbingly boring. It took me two hours to cover this section, which had little in the way of distractions, unless you count the clouds of little black flies, which stuck to my sun cream. Added to that was the heat – it was over 30°C and because the dyke was lined by trees on either side, there was no breeze of any variety to cool me down. I pedalled on and on and on, only stopping a couple of times – once to photograph the autumn crocus flowers that abounded on the slopes of the dyke and once to make a quick video. I was also hungry and thirsty – it was past 3pm now and I'd had nothing to eat since the border, although I had emptied my bidons and eaten an "emergency" flapjack.

Finally, the wetlands ended on the outskirts of Vienna with the arrival of a huge oil storage depot. I rode through the industrial complex, underneath pipelines that crossed from one side of the road to the other, crossed over a railway line and I was back by the side of the river. Almost as if my prayers had been heard, immediately afterwards there was a restaurant! I abandoned my bicycle and went to the hatchway and ordered two bottles of coke and a lángos. I drank one bottle of coke almost without taking a breath and relished my lángos and the second bottle when it arrived.

After half an hour, it was time to move on. I was now level with Vienna, but on the north bank of the Danube, whereas the city lies primarily on the southern bank. I'd covered just over 80 miles so far, but I didn't want to stay in Vienna tonight and wanted to get to the other side of the city. I settled on Klosterneuburg, because that was just north of Vienna and seemed like a reasonable target for the say. With that in mind, I fired out an Airbnb reservation for that evening.

I continued on the cycle path, past more and more restaurants and cafes, it seems this side of the river is popular as a leisure destination with many activities available, as well as those that were just enjoying the sunshine by the river.

Crossing the river again on the cycle bridge next to the Nordbrücke, I successfully negotiated the spaghetti junction of bike paths and headed out of the city. This was where I started to see the first of many river cruisers, undoubtedly disgorging hundreds of passengers for guided tours of Vienna. These boats were to become a regular sight along the remaining stretch of the Danube and at times I couldn't help thinking that they would be a far easier option.

The bike path continued, now northwards, squeezed between and sometimes even under, the railway and the busy highway, passing marinas, yacht clubs and upmarket apartments, all lining the riverside. I was approaching what I thought would be the end of my day, after 9 hours of riding when I heard the message tone on my phone. I stopped and checked it – it was not good news. "Your request to stay has been rejected". That was all. Oh great.

I had a look at other options, but Klosterneuburg didn't seem to have many options, especially options that didn't require back-tracking. I changed tack and sent out some requests to BeWelcome hosts in Tulln am der Donau. It was only 10 miles or so further on and might result in something. If not, I could always book a hotel.

The bike route continued right by the side of the river for a while before crossing a causeway to an island in the middle of the river. There was a park there and I stopped to take a photograph of Greifenstein castle atop the hill. Castles on top of hills were also going to be a regular occurrence for a while. I rode through some woods back towards the Danube again and as I emerged from the trees I could see a huge dam in front of me. This was the Greifenstein hydro-electric power plant, opened in 1985 and generating approximately 1,753 Gwh of electricity a year. It's also equipped with two locks for the Danube river cruisers and other boat traffic.

There was a levee now, along which I rode, also popular with other recreational bike riders. More yacht clubs and marinas and shortly afterwards I was arriving at Tulln. I'd had no more notifications, so I didn't know whether I had anywhere to stay or not, which was a little concerning. Then I saw a sign - "Donaupark Camping Tulln" and I thought to myself, "You know what? It's not too late. I have a tent, I'll just stop here."

A quick about-turn and I rode down the embankment and through the front gate to the reception. The lady at the reception spoke perfect English and in no time we'd established that the campsite had all the important facilities (a shower, a restaurant and a bar), so I paid my 16 Euros and went off to pitch my tent.

There were a few cyclists in the camping area, and I picked a spot where I could erect my little tent and propped my bike against a convenient tree. In no time at all, my tent was up, so I grabbed my wash bag and headed off to the showers. I did my usual routine, dressed in my shorts and tee shirt and hung my cycling clothes to try on a washing line outside. I set off to where I thought the lady had said there was a restaurant, but all I found was a small place serving snacks and beer. I wanted something a bit more substantial, so I asked a member of staff what was nearby. She recommended the tennis club, adding that the food was very good, so I walked out of the gate and down the road to find it. It wasn't far away, and I am happy to confirm that the food was indeed very good, as was the beer!

Back up the road to the campsite I had a few minutes to upload a video and a few posts on Facebook and then I curled up inside my sleeping bag and went to sleep.

## DAY 7 – TULLN TO ENNS

108 miles.

Awake at 5.30am again, although I'd been awoken a few times during the night by my neighbours. One of them kept talking in his sleep and another (or possibly the same one) kept turning over on his air bed quite noisily. I still slept OK though, so I was ready to go. The cafe at the campsite wasn't open until 7.30, so yet again I'd have to pick up some breakfast on the road. It was a lot colder this morning – about 12°C, positively chilly in comparison to the 30°C of yesterday. It also felt a lot damper, so initially I had almost all my cycling tops on, plus my arm warmers.

I packed all my stuff back in my panniers and checked that all my gear was charged. Up until now I had just plugged everything in to charge where I'd been staying, but that obviously wasn't possible in a tent. I had a couple of battery packs with me though, so I plugged my phone in to one and my GPS in the other. I could then charge the battery packs up as I rode along from my dynamo hub and a natty little gadget that converted the power from my hub to USB.

I was back on the bike path next to the river in no time and through Tulln and out the other side in ten minutes. The EV6 then tracked inland for about 5 miles to avoid a patch of marshland (and the Donau chemical plant) before emerging back by the riverside. A little further on, I passed by the Zwentendorf Nuclear Power Plant, which was built in the 1970's, but owing to a referendum in 1978 never entered service. It is now used for security training and has occasionally been used as a film location.

I then disappeared in to a forested area for a while, before popping out again on the Danube, this time at the Altenwörth Hydroelectric power plant, the most powerful power plant on the Danube, according to the Verbund website, with an annual output of 2,004,196 Mwh, which commenced operations in 1976. It also boasts Lower Austria's longest fish pass. Apparently.

The route then continued along the levee of the Danube for the next ten miles or so, in a scene very similar to yesterday. I hoped that it wasn't going to be a similar experience as yesterday, because that was no fun. It was also windier again today – not a particularly strong wind, but a constant 5 or 10 mph headwind blowing down the valley.

The route turned inland again briefly giving me a beautiful view of Göttweig Abbey, a Benedictine monastery on a hill, then taking me through Mautern an der Donau. I'd ridden 30 miles and it was just gone 9am, so I was well overdue some breakfast. I spotted a supermarket and popped in to see what I could find. The choice wasn't brilliant, so I grabbed a sandwich, an iced coffee and some chocolate and sat outside and ate. Almost as soon as I set off again, I passed through the centre of the town and spotted "Tony's Cafe", which looked like it had a lot nicer fare. Unfortunately you have to grab food when you can.

I then passed through the village of Hundsheim, which in my head I translated to "dogs home", although quite where it acquired that name I have no idea. However, I thought it would be a good place to stop for a few moments and make a video update.

From Hundsheim the route wound its way right alongside the Danube, which was beautiful and was what I had actually envisaged. The next few miles offered so many photo opportunities I thought I'd better stop taking snaps, or I'd never get anywhere. From the southern bank I had a panoramic view of the northern bank with views of towns and villages with ornate churches and red-tiled roofs, against a backdrop of cliffs or perhaps vineyards. At Arnsdorf I wanted to take a picture of Dürnstein, across the river, but there seemed to be preparations underway for some kind of concert, as they had erected a stage and there were people everywhere preparing. The bike path was "closed", but I did my usual trick of ignoring the signs and proceeded until I was stopped by a security guard. I explained to him that all I wanted to do was take a photograph and he kindly escorted me to the riverside so I could accomplish my mission.

After Arnsdorf the route cut off a serpentine curve and passed through Rossatz, winding through a vineyard and orchards. It was stunning, just stunning. Just as I passed through Rührsdorf, I met a group of cyclists heading the other way, who were quite obviously Brazilian, from their attire.

"Boa tarde!", I shouted to them, in my best Portuguese.

"Boa tarde! como vai você?" came the reply, almost in unison.

I stopped and had a conversation with them in a mix of my poor Portuguese and their (somewhat better) English. They were from São Paulo and on a Danube river cruise, but had opted to ride this section on hire bikes. I saw this a few times on different sections of the Danube – occasionally I'd see crowds of tourists heading downstream on e-bikes, presumably to rendezvous with the river cruisers further down the Danube.

The river meandered to the north and south and the EV6 carried on alongside it, occasionally next to the road, but mostly on the bank. After 50 miles and five and a half hours on the road I arrived at the town of Melk, with its 11$^{th}$ century Abbey built high above the town. It was about time I stopped for a break, although I didn't fancy lunch yet, so I settled for a coffee and a piece of Schwarzwälder Kirschtorte (black forest gateau). I remember the phrase from many many years ago whilst studying German from the BBC Deutsch Direkt! book and it seemed funny to be able to use it, all these years later.

I took a few photos of the buildings and cobbled streets around the square and set off back down the hill again, just as hoards of tourists approached from the other direction – a river cruiser must have just docked. Sure enough, as I rode back down to the river, there was a jetty, with a couple of boats alongside.

Today was nowhere near as warm as yesterday, only 18 or 20 degrees centigrade and the sky was overcast all day. In a way, this was welcome, but what was not so welcome was the wind, which was becoming very tiresome, especially on some of the longer, straighter sections of levee when heading due west. I pulled in to a small jetty at Krummnußbaum for a bit of respite from the wind and spoke to another cyclist who was there. He was riding downstream though and hadn't even noticed the wind, as it helped him on his way.

I looped south on another curve in the river and rode through Ybbs an der Donau, another pretty town which delayed me a little while taking photographs. I was getting hungry now and it was about lunchtime, so I had been looking for somewhere convenient to eat. I had seen a number of cafes all along the river, but the vast majority of them were closed. I had been warned by other EuroVelo riders that this might be the case this late in the season. I could probably have found somewhere open in Ybbs, had I diverted away from the bike route, but I imagined I'd spot somewhere open sooner or later. "Somewhere" appeared sooner, rather than later in the form of a Wirtshaus in Donaudorf. To be honest, it didn't look very open, but it said open on the door. I pushed my bike up a ramp on to a verandah, wandered over to the hatchway, but that was closed. Just as I was about to get on my bike and ride off, a woman came out and started shouting at me in German, obviously upset about something. Eventually I understood that I'd pushed my bike up the wheelchair ramp, which was obviously verboten. I did find her demeanour a bit strange, given that I was the only person there. I did manage to establish that the place was open though, so I walked in, to what looked like somebody's dining room. I ordered a currywurst and fries and a coke and sat at the table. The TV was on, so I had probably interrupted her afternoon viewing? Eventually a one-eyed gentleman appeared with my food, which was very tasty and I sat and ate my lunch quietly while the lady watched TV. As soon as I'd finished, I paid my bill and left. All in all, a very odd experience.

I had clocked up 75 miles now, so 25 miles to my daily "target" mileage. There didn't appear to be a large number of towns along the next stretch of the river though, the next larger settlement being Enns. The only problem with that, was that it was the other side of the river by the same name. There was a passenger ferry, but my concern now was that it might not be running. I guess I would find out when I got there. I suppose there was always the tent.

Some of the next sections of the river were closed to general traffic, just access and bicycles. The valley was narrower here and forested on either side. There was a main road on the far side of the river and I could see plenty of traffic on it, so it was very pleasant to be on the quiet side. There were a few small villages through which I passed and one or two cars, but mostly I had the road to myself. As I rode alongside the river, I caught up with one of the many commercial barges that run up and down the Danube. It was obviously motoring along at a decent speed, because it took me quite a while to overtake it.

The road reappeared at Hößgang, opposite the pretty town of Grein, once again with Schloß Greinburg sitting atop a hill. Just as I was almost in danger of Schloß overload, the EV6 looped inland, away from the river through a patchwork of fields, returning to the river a few miles later at Wallsee, next to the Donaukraftwerk Wallsee-Mitterkirchen hydro-electric plant. The bike path ran along the top of a levee for a few miles, then once again headed away from the river.

The road weaved left and right through fields, woods and small villages and seemed to go on forever. Occasionally I could see raised hides, which I assumed to be more likely used for shooting than bird watching. I hardly saw any traffic – in fact, I hardly saw anything until I arrived in Sankt Pantaleon-Erka, where I caught up with a couple of other people riding bikes. I'm not sure if they were e-bikes or not (though e-bikes seemed incredibly popular in Austria, Germany and the Netherlands, much more so than in the UK), but they took some catching. Of course I had the excuse of having ridden for eleven hours. Just after I had caught them, I rode up a bank to the top of the levee again whereas they stayed on the road and disappeared off in to the distance. I didn't see them again. I had to cut inland again to cross a small canal, before passing through an underpass and down a gravel track to the river. The weekend had obviously started for a number of people, because the track was lined with cars and there were lots of people fishing. The river bank turned away from the Danube – this must be the Enns river – all I had to do now was find the ferry terminal.

I use the word "terminal" lightly, because when I found it, it was no more than a gangway, with a small floating jetty at the bottom. There was nobody else there, but more to the point there was no ferry either.

I began reading the sign, attempting to translate the German for a while, when I saw the English translation on the other side. That was handy. My brain wasn't in the right gear for anything complicated. The first thing I noticed was the operation times – May to August 9:00 to 19:00, September 9:00 to 18:00. It was 17:33. Phew!

I called the telephone number displayed and a man answered in German.

"Sprechen Sie Englisch?", I tried…

"Yes", he replied. Phew again.

"I'm at the bike ferry terminal", I said.

"Which one?", he asked. I didn't really know, to be honest. It seems that I had three options, Enns, Mauthausen or St. Pantaleon, looking at the sign. Then I remembered, I'd just ridden past Sankt Pantaleon, although it was a while back.

"Uhh… Sankt Pantaleon", I replied.

"OK, I'll be there in five minutes", he said.

I wheeled my bike down the aluminium gangway on to the pontoon, being as careful as I could. The last thing I needed was for my bike or myself to end up on the bottom of the Danube. A few minutes later, a vessel loomed in to view that had the aspect of a garden shed sitting on top of a landing craft. The driver had obviously made this manoeuvre many times though, as he skilfully navigated the craft up to the jetty and lowered the ramp. Without further ado, I wheeled my bike on to the launch and we were away.

Along with the pilot, there were a lady and child, who were making the trip from Mauthausen to Enns, with a diversion to collect me. I paid my fare and asked the pilot if he could recommend somewhere to stay, and he replied with the "Goldenen Schiff" (the Golden Ship). Google suggested this was about 20 minutes away, so with the Golden Ship set as my destination, I disembarked and headed off.

It seemed like a long 20 minutes to the centre of Enns, but Google got me there eventually and after a couple of laps of the square I found the hotel, just next to a Gelateria. I dumped my bike outside and walked through the entrance, to find the owner busy working away in the side passage. I explained to him that the man on the Radfähre had recommended him and in no time at all I was booked in.

The hotelier showed me my room and said I could put my bike in the side passage, where there were already some more, which I duly did. I detached my bags and went to my room, showered and changed.

That evening, I fancied a pizza and just across the square I found "Pizzeria Stadt Linz". How convenient! In I walked and was offered a table. It wasn't terribly busy, so it wasn't long before I was served. I tried the same routine:

"Sprechen Sie Englisch?"

"Nein", the young lady replied. Oh dear. Out of wishful thinking more than anything else I tried:

"Spanisch?"

"Ja" – this was looking much better. I ordered a beer and a spicy pizza. When the lady returned, I asked her how come she spoke Spanish so well.

"Well", she replied (in Spanish), "I'm Romanian, but I worked for a long time in Spain…"

What a turn-up for the books… I explained that I was cycling from Romania to England and that I had a Romanian dog. I don't know if she was just making polite conversation, but we chatted for a while about this and that before long my pizza was ready. I polished off my pizza in no time and pulled out my phone to pay, only to discover that cards and Google Pay wasn't accepted. I found this more and more throughout Austria and Germany (especially in the south), where obviously cash is king. Luckily there was a Sparkasse bank next door, so I nipped out and got some Euros out of the machine to pay. I then went out and wandered around the pretty square, taking in the atmosphere. There was just time for a video update for Facebook before I headed back to the hotel for my customary video call with Jill and off to bed.

*Ybbs an der Donau*

# Day 8 – Enns to Passau

75 miles.

Today was a Sunday, so obviously a good day for a lie-in. I didn't really have a lie-in though, as I was still awake early. Nothing to do until breakfast though, so I packed everything up as much as possible so I could make a hasty exit as soon as I could. I went downstairs as soon as breakfast might be ready and was soon tucking in to muesli, yoghurt, fruit, pastries and quite frankly everything I could lay my hands on. I can heartily recommend the "Goldenen Schiff" and its breakfast!

Once I'd eaten my fill, I returned to my room and got changed. I applied a liberal dollop of chamois cream to my shorts, as I'd been having some "issues" in that area. I grabbed my kit and went back downstairs to my bike.

I met the hotelier again and thanked him for his service, remarking that the man on the Radfähre had made an excellent recommendation.

"He should", replied the hotelier, "I own the Radfähre too…"

Finally, I asked him where I could get some water for my bidons. He took me behind the bar and showed me a pump marked "wasser". He pointed out that the one next to it was "Weißwein" and suggested that the latter might be a grave mistake. Hmm. Water or wine in my bottles...

Outside it was shaping up to be another lovely day – blue skies and sunshine, but not too hot, only in the high teens. I did a couple of laps around the square again so my GPS could sort itself out and before long I was heading out of Enns in to the countryside. After 30 minutes I was back at the Danube and crossing it on another hydro electric plant. I was now on the north bank of the river, flying along once more on a perfectly surfaced bike path. It wasn't long before I could see the industrial sprawl of Linz in front of me.

Linz is a very industrial city and the "industrial sprawl" I could see as I cycled up the river was mainly the Voestalpine steelworks at the confluence of the rivers Danube and Traun. Voestalpine was founded as the "Reichswerke Hermann Göring" in 1937. Right next door to the steel plant is the Königswinter hot rolling plant, that rolls steel in to plates. The other side of the Steyregg Bridge is Linz Chemical park, an industrial park that is home to a number of chemical industry companies. From the other side of the river I could see a number of the industrial barges moored next to the steelworks. According to Pro Danube, "the voice for better infrastructure and innovation in Danube transport", "More than 40 million tons of goods were carried on the Danube waterway and its tributaries in 2014", although further investigation reveals this had been in decline since then.

The rather more picturesque centre of Linz is some five miles further upstream and around a bend in the river, past the huge cable-stayed Vöest road bridge, with its nine lanes of traffic, and the steel Neue Eisenbahnbrücke (New Railway Bridge), which despite the name is also a road bridge now. Moored up alongside the bank now were the river cruisers, this section of the city being rather more attractive than the steelworks…

I had a bit of a navigational error at the Nibelungen Bridge a little further on, where I thought the route climbed from the river bank up to the bridge up a steep zig-zag ramp, but upon reaching the top my GPS beeped at me and said "Off course – make a u-turn", sending me back down the ramp to the river bank again and under the bridge. Shortly later I heard a "ping" on my phone and stopped to see what it was. It was Jill.

*Can you order me some poo bags please...*

Lovely. I ordered some poo bags from the riverside, and took a photograph of the Westring Bridge, a new suspension bridge  under construction for the Linz west ring (A26), which involves blasting through the rock on either side of the river.

Five miles further on I arrived at Ottensheim, where my route crossed the Danube again, this time on a ferry. To be precise, there were options for the EV6 on both sides of the Danube, but I'd chosen the south bank for this stretch. The Ottensheim ferry was on the far bank when I arrived, so I waited and enjoyed the sunshine while it travelled across. The ferry is a "reaction" ferry, a cable ferry that uses the reaction of the current of a river against a fixed tether to propel the vessel across the water. It didn't take long to cross and drop its ramp and as soon as the ferry passengers had disembarked I wheeled my bike down the ramp. I paid my fare and soon the ferry departed. Although the ferry was a reaction ferry, since the construction of the Ottensheim-Wilhering hydro electric plant a couple of miles upstream the flow of the river wasn't sufficient to cast off without the assistance of an engine, but as soon as we were underway, the engine stopped and we drifted peacefully across the rest of the river.

After disembarking on the south bank, the next ten miles or so once again were riding along a raised levee. In due course, near the village of Brandstatt I spied a kiosk at the side of the river. I was three hours and 30 miles in to the day, so it seemed like an excellent moment to make a stop. I sat in the sun at the side of the river and ordered a coke, a coffee and an apple strudel – I was in Austria, after all!

I fired off a message to our Facebook group with a photo of my apple strudel with the Danube in the background.

*Me: Lovely today. If only my bum didn't hurt...*

I sent a picture of a cloud, which looked like a dog.

*Ann: You're hallucinating...*

Well, at least *I* thought it looked like a dog.

Three or four miles further up the river, just past the next hydro-electric dam, once again the road was closed to motor vehicles and remained this way for something like the next 20 miles! Those 20 miles were probably the most enjoyable 20 miles of the entire trip. That section of the Danube meanders through a steep-sided, tree-lined valley almost completely devoid of any settlements. I was far from on my own though, almost all the way there was a constant stream of tourists on bikes and e-bikes cycling downstream – this must be a popular option on the river cruise circuit and I can see why. At one point I made a video while riding along the bike path:

"This is what I envisaged, when I envisaged riding the Danube cycle path. It's just beautiful. Stunning. The path is brilliant, the scenery is fantastic, you couldn't wish for more…"

I stopped at the village of Schlögen for a bite to eat, then crossed the river to the north bank once more on a small ferry. The north bank was just as pretty as the south bank, although the road reappeared again at the 52 mile mark, it was still only a single-track road, with more cyclists than motor vehicles. I stopped for an ice-cream in a village called Kramesau and managed to re-apply some more chamois cream. Even the saddle-sores weren't spoiling my day that much! Then, without any fanfare, almost without noticing it, I was in Germany.

*Passau, Germany*

# Chapter 11. Germany

Gradually the valley widened and civilization reappeared at the town of Obernzell. There was still little traffic though, almost rendering the excellent bike path unnecessary. The bike paths were still there though and I continued to use them, because, well, why wouldn't I?

In due course, I could see my destination for the day, Passau. The city lies on a peninsula at the confluence of the rivers Inn, Ilz and the Danube. As I approached the city, it was the old town on this peninsula that I could see first, with it's colourful buildings and ever-present river-cruisers. I had nowhere booked, so I pulled over to the side of the road and pulled out my phone. I followed the usual procedure – hotel app, pick the cheapest, which on this occasion turned out to be a "Limehome" apartment in Bahnhofstraße, near the station. I booked it up and carried on towards the city.

It was only a couple of miles to the apartment and after I'd managed to negotiate the bridge over the river Iln, the tunnel through the headland and the Prince Regent Luitpold Bridge over the Danube it was a short ride down the promenade (past yet more river-cruisers) to my destination. On arrival, rather than a reception of some variety I found myself outside the door of an apartment block. In the meantime, I'd received an email, saying that I needed to "perform my check-in online" and that I would then be sent the key code for the door and further instructions. This is where things started to go pear-shaped. I clicked on the link in the email, my browser opened and did nothing. I was eventually presented with an error page that said "No Internet". Great!

I wandered up the street in search of a better signal, but it didn't seem to help. MacDonalds, I thought. They always have free WiFi, I'll find a MacDonalds and do it there. Unfortunately, I had no idea where MacDonalds was and I couldn't look it up on the map, because I had no Internet. I wasn't quite sure what was going on, because even in the depths of Romania, or on the Hungarian plains I had no issues, but here, in a major city in Bavaria, I was stuck.

A little further up the street I still had no signal, so I asked some ladies:

"Entschuldigen Sie bitte, gibt es in der Nähe einen MacDonald's?"

From the glazed look on their faces I could sense this was going to be difficult. I could smell alcohol and they looked a bit worse for wear. I did manage to understand that yes, there was a MacDonald's, but it was nowhere nearby. I bade them farewell and went on my way. Just then, I saw a nearby fast food restaurant and thought I'd try there. I asked if they had WiFi, but the young lady replied no. I explained my predicament and very kindly she offered to share her mobile Internet so I could check in.

Once I'd connected to her mobile hot spot, I tried the website again and this time managed to connect. I had to put in my surname and the code that I'd been emailed. I did exactly that, but got an error – "invalid code". I tried again – same error. I was getting more and more frustrated, so in desperation I called the helpline number. In all fairness, the helpline was very helpful. I could speak to someone in English and we ascertained that their system had my forename and surname swapped around. Undoubtedly, if I'd put "Steven" and the code, I might have got somewhere. Anyway, the gentleman swapped me around and sent me the code for the door via email.

I rode back to the door, entered the code and buzzed myself in. The apartment was on the third floor, but I just managed to squeeze my bike in the lift and went up. Now, the email mentioned that I needed to find a key box, punch in a different code and get the keys. I found a key box, punched in the code, but it didn't work! At this point I vowed never to use Limehome ever again… I called the helpline once more and spoke to a lady this time. After a while, she discovered that in *this* Limehome, there *wasn't* actually a keybox and that there was an electronic keypad on the door, on which I had to had to punch first a 5-digit code, then a 4-digit code. Nothing, if not complicated. Finally, I managed to get indoors. It had taken me over an hour since I first arrived at the door. All I could think, was that thankfully I'd only ridden 75 miles today and had arrived relatively early.

I showered, changed and went back to the restaurant to thank the young lady once more and scoffed down the biggest burger on the menu. Afterwards, I went out in to the old town, grabbed an ice-cream from a gelateria and wandered around taking in the surroundings. It is indeed, a beautiful city. What a shame I had to waste so much time on the hotel debacle.

Back at the apartment I made myself a coffee from the machine, sat on the bed and updated social media with today's news and fell asleep in front of the TV.

# DAY 9 – PASSAU TO REGENSBURG

96 miles.

Yet again I was awake at an indecent hour and there was no breakfast to look forward to here, so I had one of my sachets of porridge and a coffee and packed up ready to go. I shuttled my bike downstairs in the lift again and left the building. It was cold this morning, 7°C at 6.30am, and I was wearing just about everything, including my down jacket. By the end of the day it was up to the high 20's, but for the time being I even needed my warm gloves.

I fired up my GPS, loaded the route and headed of town on Regensburger Strasse. I had literally ridden a couple of miles, when I came to the "Laufwasserkraftwerk Kachlet" hydroelectric dam, where I was supposed to cross the Danube. Unfortunately, it was closed, with a big sign saying "Asbestsanierung" (Asbestos removal). Given that the dam was built in 1927, it's hardly surprising that it may have contained asbestos, but this was a sign of how the day was going to continue. The Kachlet dam was originally built to overcome a dangerously shallow section of the Danube, which made it difficult to navigate. It didn't help my navigation much.

Google maps showed me that the next upstream bridge was a motorway bridge, so that wasn't an option. The next downstream bridge was a railway bridge, then there was the Franz-Josef-Strauß-Brücke. I didn't know if this bridge allowed bicycles, plus it was elevated high above the river and Regensburger Strasse and I wasn't sure how I was going to get up to it. I back-tracked my route and eventually decided that my best option was to ride up the pavement on the exit slip road and see if I could cross. Just as approached the top of the exit ramp, I was passed by a cyclist riding in the opposite direction, so it looked as if I was lucky.

Back on the other side of the Danube, I soon found my original route and headed west. I rode along the bike path parallel to the main road for a while, then ducked through an underpass and headed out in to the countryside by the river. Just as I passed below the motorway bridge, I saw a man walking across the road in swimming trunks with a towel over his shoulder. There was a boat ramp nearby I I expect he was going for a morning dip in the river, but at 7°C he was obviously made of sterner stuff than me!

The path stayed alongside the river and passed fields and small villages. After about an hour on the road, the sun started to rise behind me, with a beautiful pink hue above the shallow fog. There was a similar shallow fog over the river too, so I stopped briefly to take a couple of photos.

I continued on my way; sometimes a road appeared on my right, but it was quiet at this time of the morning and there was always a cycle path. I was progressing well and in a couple of hours I'd reached the town of Winzer. It was time for my first break and I spotted a bakery just as I entered town. I soon got used to the fact that bakeries opened early in Germany and often served coffee too. This one had an exceptional range of bread and pastries, so I sat and enjoyed my second breakfast and it wasn't even 9am yet.

The Danube started to meander here and my route cut across some loops, through the fields, turning left, then right, then left. Sometimes I popped out alongside the river, or rode by a levee bordering it for a while, then the EV6 might deviate through a village or small town for a while, past white-fronted houses with red-tiles roofs. Things were going well, until I reached the town of Metten. Here, the EV6 was closed – I'm not sure why, but the barriers made it perfectly clear. I diverted off the bike path and on to the main road for a short while, before I jumped on to another bike path that took me in to the town of Metten. I was clearly heading the wrong way though, because the sun was at my back, meaning I was heading north, not west. This diversion obviously wasn't working for me, so I crossed a small bridge and headed south again. This took me back to the EV6, but it was still closed. I turned around and went back to the road and turned left along the main road, not great, but at least I was heading in the right direction. Then, after about a mile, the road was closed as well, with a sign directing all the traffic on to the Autobahn. This obviously wasn't an option for me, so I dodged the "road closed" signs and carried on. Shortly I could see why the road was closed, as there was obviously a major upgrade in progress. Fortunately, although the EV6 was "closed", there wasn't actually any work being undertaken on the EV6 itself, so I was able to scramble up the bank to the bike path and ride along it, looking down at the heavy machinery at work on the road.

That obstacle overcome, I carried on for another three or four miles and the same thing happened again. This time though, the work seemed to be on the EV6 itself, so there was no option but to divert away from the river and through the village of Loham. These roads weren't busy though, so it wasn't a huge problem, apart from the constant beeping from my GPS telling me I was off course. The road I followed for the next few miles was actually a bike route and truth be told it actually cut across a loop in the river, so technically you might have called it a short cut.

It was now lunchtime – well, to be honest it was a little early for lunchtime, but I didn't think I could last the extra hour until Straubing, so I thought I'd see if there was anywhere open in Bogen. I didn't have long to wait, as I saw an Italian restaurant almost immediately as I entered the pretty town square. I could see it was open too, as there were a couple of men sitting outside with a beer, I thought it was a little early for beer, but I suppose the "sun was over the yardarm". I abstained from alcohol and stuck with a very tasty bowl of pasta instead. Before I left I went to the bathroom and applied another dollop of chamois cream to my nether regions and made a mental note that I was getting pretty short now and would have to see if I could buy some more.

Straubing had a couple of bike shops, as far as I could see, so while I had considered cutting that loop out of the EV6 to save some miles, I thought it might be best to see if they stocked chamois cream instead. The river splits in two at Straubing, with the city on the bank of the southern loop. I crossed the first bridge, then looked out for the first bike shop, "Dein perfektes Rad" (your perfect bike). It was a fairly large shop, so I was hopeful, but it wasn't something they stocked. I crossed the second bridge and went through the city gates in to the old town. I quickly found the second bike shop, but it didn't look like the right kind of place, so didn't go in. In a way I was glad I hadn't cut the loop off, because if I had, I would have missed a very pretty detour, although the cobbled streets didn't do my saddle sores much good.

I crossed back over the Danube again at another dam and hydroelectric power station, though a small one in comparison to those further downstream. Back out in to the countryside I continued along the EuroVelo 6, zig-zagging through the countryside again through the fields. There was a fairly long section along a levee with a gravel surface right next to the river which was a bit bumpy, but it was also very light, almost white in colour. Even though I had my sunglasses on the reflected sunlight was very strong and I could feel the heat of the sun on my face. It all became a bit much near Wörth an der Donau and I sat down in the shade under a bridge for a while to have a rest and a drink from my bidon.

These last few days I could feel the effect of the distance. Generally I felt OK in the morning, but as the day wore on and the sun took its toll, self doubt began to set in. I tried to boost myself by singing a bit. As I was in Germany I tried a bit of Rammstein (in Austria I had sung tunes from "The Sound of Music") but it didn't work. I then moved on to a bit of d-i-s-c-o, which never failed to work. I never ride with headphones, as many of my friends do, but I always have some tune buzzing around inside my head and I often hum along, or sing, if I can remember the words. I think I shocked a van driver in Germany at some point, as I flew past him singing about killing a man, putting a gun against his head…

Closer towards Regensburg my phone rang, which I thought was a bit odd. I couldn't answer it in time, but I called back and it was BBC Hereford and Worcester, who wanted to do a spot on Amicii and Stella's Journey. I chatted to the researcher for a little while and they wanted to call me back at 4.20pm, or 5.20 my time. I said that should be OK, as I should be in Regensburg by then – I'd better get a move on though, I thought. I was still 30km away, according to the latest signpost, although I'm pretty sure I saw a signpost about 15 minutes earlier that also said 30km!

I'd arranged to stay with a couple that night via bewelcome.org, so as I arrived at the outskirts of Regensburg, I cancelled my GPS route and plugged the address of their apartment block to Google. It wasn't that far away, but it was a little tricky as I had to cross a couple of Danube bridges and I went wrong a couple of times. It would have been a lot easier if I had a handlebar mount for my phone – note for future trips.

After about 25 minutes I arrived outside the address and was met at the door by my host. She led me down in to the underground car park where I could safely store my bike, before we headed to their apartment, where I met her partner and their Border Collie, Dorie. I explained about the interview and I was offered a shower first and the opportunity to wash my clothes, both of which I gratefully accepted.

Duly showered and changed, we chatted for a short while before my phone rang and I was live on air! I chatted with Andrew Easton on his evening drive time show for a few minutes, explaining the reasons behind my ride and hopefully increasing the visibility a little more.

With my five minutes of fame over, all four of us (Dorie included!) walked in to the town centre where I treated my guests to dinner. We enjoyed a beer and some great food together, before my hosts were off to an open mic concert, where they hoped to be able to sing a song they'd been practising. I too was invited, but at 9pm I was almost falling asleep in my Kartoffelsalat, so I graciously declined. I strolled back to their apartment, let myself in and was asleep on the couch within minutes.

*Sheltering from the sun...*

# DAY 10 – REGENSBURG TO ROTHENBURG

112 miles.

Awake at 5am this morning and on the road at 6.09. I crept out of the apartment after retrieving my (still damp) clothing from the washing line. I didn't want to wake my guests as I didn't know what time they got back last night, but they didn't disturb me. I let myself out and walked down to the garage where my bike was waiting, hooked on my panniers and I was off. My GPS had some disagreements about which was the best way to pick up the EV6, so I ignored it which sometimes seems the best thing to do.

It was only a couple of miles to the Großprüfunging railway bridge, where I crossed the Danube for the last time. Today was a big day, because today I left the Danube, which I had been following for the last 500 miles or so, to cut across Germany to the Rhine and EuroVelo 15, which I would follow all the way to Hook of Holland. I had planned two days for this next section of about 230 miles and was a bit worried I might have bitten off more than I could chew. Unlike riding up the Danube, the next two days were going to be hilly, containing the bulk of all the climbing for the entire trip. The climbing didn't take long to appear, and after only five miles I hit the hill at Etterzhausen. There was no way I was going to be able to cycle up it, so I capitulated early and walked.

Amazingly, after only seven miles I spotted a bakery in Nittendorf that was open, so I popped in for breakfast. I had some of my usual kaffee und kuchen from the excellent selection available. I commented to the lady behind the counter on how cold it was this morning to which she replied "Ja! Summer is over!"

After Nittendorf the road continued to climb, until after Hernau I'd climbed over 2000 feet and had a beautiful view of the Bavarian countryside. I stopped to take some photos, as everything seemed so perfect – green fields, blue skies, houses with red-tiles roofs, picturesque churches, perfect roads. This part of Bavaria is quite sparsely populated though as I found out later when I asked a couple of ladies if there was anywhere nearby I might buy a drink. It seems as if there are no local shops at all, everyone preferring to top up at the nearest supermarket instead. This presented a bit of a problem for me, as I was unable to find anywhere to stop for my 25-mile break, so I just stopped at a crossroads and ate something I'd saved from earlier.

My routing was also a little bit experimental today – some of the roads I'd chosen some weeks earlier proved to be nothing more than forest tracks and although I didn't mind a little bit of off-road, I was too heavily loaded to do long stretches. Some stretches were unavoidable though, such as the one dropping down through the forest to Mühlhausen, as an asphalted detour would have been too far. At Mühlhausen I had to divert in to the town centre to a supermarket, as I didn't know how far it might be to the next place I could get something to eat and drink. As well as food and drink, I also managed to pick up a tin of baby cream, which I thought might suffice as chamois cream, as I was now running perilously low.

As it turned out, I'd have probably been OK, because only a few miles further on I passed through the town of Freystadt. I didn't stop, but I poked my nose through the gate of the old town and was rewarded with a cobbled square, lined with pastel colour houses of typical Bavarian style, with steeply pitched roofs and and timbered walls.

A couple of miles later, I was riding alongside a canal – the Rhine–Main–Danube Canal. This canal, as its name suggests connects the river Main to the Danube, which provides a navigable route all the way from the North Sea to the Black Sea.

I could have done with finding somewhere for lunch now, but instead of sensibly heading to the centre of Roth, where I'm sure I would have found somewhere, I continued on my route, hoping that I would come across something. There was nowhere I passed in Rothaurach that was open – there was a bakery, but it had closed at 1pm. Then my route diverted me a couple of miles up a a forest track before I had to turn around and back-track due to forestry operations preventing me from going any further. I felt pretty low at this point, as I'd been cycling for 63 miles and over seven hours, with nothing much to eat in quite a while. I sat on a bench at Aurau under the sparse shade of a small tree and ate and drank what I had.

I managed to pick up some more food and drink a few miles on in Abenberg which cheered me up a little, but by Wassermungenau I was well and truly cheesed off again. My route had sent me up a cart track before I abandoned it and turned back to the road. I had nobody to blame but myself – I mustn't have been paying attention when I mapped this section out. It was almost 3pm and I still had more than 40 miles to go. I decided to abandon my pre-planned route and take as direct a route to Rothenburg as I could. I picked the Google route, as these generally aren't too bad, although I did have a pretty bad time in France many years ago, when Google insisted on sending me through fields. On this occasion it wasn't too bad, and I started to make some progress. I wasn't so keen on the route it picked through Ansbach though, as it chose to send me right through the centre on, or rather next to the dual carriageway.

My new route carried on in the same vein, mostly alongside main roads on the bike path until it finally departed from them at Colmberg and followed a local bike path instead. Some of this route wasn't metalled though and some of it appear to pass through farmyards, but nobody shouted at me, so it can't have been wrong. The day seemed to be going on forever, but the end was in sight. The final sting in the tail was a steep hill out of Aidenau, before passing through the forest and dropping down in to Neusitz. The bike path was closed as I entered Rothenburg, but I was past caring now and I just rode down the main road in to the centre. I'd booked the "China Restaurant Hotel Lotus", as it was the cheapest hotel available. I rolled up outside the door at 6.56pm, after riding for nearly 13 hours.

I locked my bike outside the door and went in to check in, which I'd done after I'd attracted the attention of the lady, who was busy serving in the restaurant. She passed me the keys to my room on the second floor and then rushed back to attend to the restaurant. I hadn't asked her where I could put my bike, but it didn't look like there was anywhere I could put it other than in my room. I grabbed my bags and took them up first, then struggled up the stairs to the second floor with my bike. I was so tired that evening that I turned on the shower and just walked in with my clothes on.

After I'd showered and changed and felt a little more human I went out to have a look and see if I could find something to eat. Just as I left my room I saw a young lady carrying her bike upstairs. I laughed and said "I'm not the only one then!" She didn't speak much English and as we already know my German is limited, so that's as far as we got.

I walked out of the hotel-restaurant in to town, looking for somewhere to eat – I could have stayed where I was, but I rather wanted something with more carbohydrates, like pasta or pizza, but the town was pretty busy and the restaurants I enquired at were all telling me to come back later. Eventually I gave up and went back to my Chinese hotel-restaurant and ordered some dim sum and sweet and sour chicken. Just as I was about to go upstairs again to bed, I spied the German lady sitting in the restaurant too. Neither of us had wanted to eat Chinese food that night, but it was the easy option. We spoke a while and both agreed that we'd have preferred to eat somewhere else! We discussed our rides and it transpired she'd ridden 160km from Darmstadt to Regensburg. I replied that I was heading for Darmstadt tomorrow. With that, I bade her goodnight and climbed the stairs to my room and hit the sack.

*Wallfahrtskirche Hl. Dreifaltigkeit – Eichlberg (Hemau)*

# DAY 11 – ROTHENBURG TO DARMSTADT

106 miles.

Another early start, I was awake at 5am – getting to be habit-forming. There was no breakfast at my Chinese restaurant/hotel, so there wasn't any point hanging around. I could have had a coffee, but although the room had mugs, there was no coffee, or tea, or even a kettle. I guess I could have fired up my camping stove and made porridge and coffee, but I imagine that would have been frowned upon, especially if the fire alarm went off.

I carried my bike and bags down the two flights of stairs as quietly as I could and stepped out in to the cold air of the morning. By late afternoon the temperature would rise to 30°C again, but at 6am it was only 8°C, so I was wearing just about all the clothes I had with me. It was still dark, so I turned on my lights and set off. I had the usual initial navigation problems with my GPS and ended up wandering around in circles for a few minutes while it figured out where I was and which way I needed to go, before making its mind up. When it had decided which way was correct, it took me down a steep hill in to the river Tauber valley and straight back up the steep hill on the other side. If I was cold setting out, I wasn't by the time I reached the top.

At the top of the hill, I left Bavaria and entered Baden-Württemberg, home to the Black Forest, although I wouldn't be going anywhere near it. The Black Forest (famous for its gateaux, obviously) is in the south-west of the state, whereas I was heading in a north-easterly direction still. After about an hour, the sun began to rise behind me and I stopped to take a photo of the sunrise. I love this time of day, especially in the summer when the weather is good. You have the roads to yourself and are often rewarded with some fantastic photographs. I was riding on minor roads; the main roads and Autobahn ran north-south here and were to the east and west of me. Also, I'd re-plotted my route last night – not easy on my phone – and this time I made sure I checked the "avoid off-road" box, so I was hoping that the revised route was going to be better than yesterday's. Certainly the road between Rothenburg and Niederstetten was shaping up well. I was riding through a patchwork of fields, interspersed with villages full of traditional timbered houses. These were also deserted at 7am in the morning, although at one point I did hear the sound of a tractor working in the fields nearby.

After a couple of hours I flew down the hill in to Niederstetten, dropping past the airport outside the town. At the bottom of the hill I checked out the town on Google to see if there was anywhere I might find breakfast. I was in luck, there was a supermarket just down the road. In a few minutes I was outside a Netto and more importantly, it had a Weber's cafe. I had got quite cold speeding down the hill in to town (it was still only 8°C, even though the sun had risen) so I was grateful for the warmth of the cafe. I took my time eating my ham and cheese sub and kuchen and allowed the coffee to warm me up a little.

I needn't have worried about warming up though, as leaving town on Bahnhofstraße the road rose 400 feet in the space of a mile. What goes up must come down though, as the old adage says and this was certainly true in this instance, as the road was pretty much downhill for the next 10 miles as I dropped back down to the river Tauber. This was the same river I'd left behind in Rothenburg and I probably could have followed it downstream to Igersheim, where I joined it now, but effectively I had cut off a corner. I continued to descent all the way to Bad Mergentheim, largely on fully-segregated cycle paths, all of which were perfectly surfaced. Occasionally, where the surface had been broken by tree roots, for example, the fault had been liberally marked with yellow paint to warn of the imperfection.

I bypassed Bad Mergentheim - although in retrospect I wish I hadn't, as I've since learnt the centre is very picturesque – and left town on the "old road" to Boxberg. Now, my GPS has a feature called "ClimbPro", which according to the blurb "is designed to help riders manage their efforts on significant climbs". Basically, it gives you a mini-preview of the upcoming hill profile, with colour-coding to show how steep it is. I'd seen a few "ClimbPro" alerts on my ride up to now, but they were mostly yellow, or orange, with small bits of red. As I reached the bottom of the Boxberg road it bleeped at me and flashed up a "ClimbPro" screen which looked absolutely terrifying. After a short section of orange, the profile went red, then black. I'm not sure I've ever seen black before. The hill stretched out in front of me in a straight line, rising 400 feet in less than ¾ of a mile. I changed down in to my granny gear before attacking the lower slopes, the orange section on my GPS. I ground away as steadily as I could, but as I approached the red section it was obviously just not going to work. I surrendered to the hill and walked the rest of the way.

At the top of the hill I stopped to strip off some of my layers; it wasn't that hot, but it was definitely warming up. I took off my leggings and overshoes anyway. I was on a bigger regional road now, a Landesstraße, but despite that, it was pretty quiet and although there was no bike path, I felt safe enough. The road went up and down for the next few miles; the up wasn't so much fun, but the down was great and I managed to get up to 35 MPH at one point! I stopped in another Netto in Schweigern for elevenses, before starting the long climb over the hills to the north-west. The next 20 miles was going to be through a sparsely populated area of farmland so I made sure my bidons were full and I had some extra food. I was glad I did, as the next couple of hours were hard work; certainly very nice cycling roads, but hot and thirsty work with little or no relief. There were a large number of wind farms, no neighbours to upset here, so probably a great place for them. I sat and made a slightly late morning update for Facebook, but typically in such areas there was no signal, so it wouldn't upload.

At about midday I dropped in to the town of Hardheim and this marked the end of this section. The next part of the route followed first the river Erf, then the river Main as far as Obernburg, so I was looking forward to a nice easy ride. For the next five miles I rode down the valley on the *Landesstraße*, which was pretty quiet all the way from Hardheim to the village of Riedern. Just before Riedern the route reverted to an excellent bike path, where I took the opportunity to sit on a park bench and strip the rest of my layers off, as the temperature was now in the low twenties. The path continued to Eichenbühl, where I stopped for lunch at 1.30pm. This area was obviously popular as a holiday destination as I passed quite a few campsites. This also meant that it was pretty easy to find somewhere for lunch and I had a very nice burger and fries at Schützenhaus Eichenbühl, along with the customary gallon of coke!

With my hunger and thirst well and truly sated I continued down the valley on the bike path, now riding past the vineyards of the Franken region of Germany. The river Elf joins the river Main at Bürgstadt, where I crossed the bridge on the road and immediately returned to the bike path again. The bike path did eventually end at Großheubach, where I passed through another beautiful cobbled square with timbered buildings; but only for a mile or so, as I then cut right down the the banks of the river Main and rode for ten miles on the purpose-built cycleway. Both sides of the river here were lined with campsites, caravans and holiday chalets and there were still plenty of people here enjoying the late September sunshine. I started to see river traffic again too, both commercial and pleasure cruisers. At Erlenbach I could see where some of these had presumably been built, as there was a shipyard right by the river. Right opposite the shipyard was the historic town of Wörth am Main, protected by a huge pair of steel flood gates. These have been thoroughly tested in recent years, as the Main valley had been subject to increasingly worse floods, including the most recent in 2021, when 196 deaths were reported across Germany. Inside the gates is the old town, with cobbled streets and timbered buildings in typical Bavarian style.

I left the river Main at Obernburg, where I needed to cut across to Darmstadt, today's destination. The Main continues south in a loop through Frankfurt, eventually joining the Rhine at Mainz, where I too would join the Rhine tomorrow. Between me and Darmstadt unfortunately, were a couple of ranges of hills and about 30 miles, which wouldn't normally present a problem, but I'd already been in the saddle for nine hours. From Obernburg I headed west up the river valley, before leaving the river at Mömlingen. Then I passed through a succession of delightful towns and villages before I arrived at the last major climb of the day, after Radheim, rising over 400 feet in a mile. I toiled up the hill in the 28 degree heat, stopping briefly in the shade on one of the serpentine bends. After the crest, I enjoyed flying down the other side of the hill so much that I missed the turning for Klein-Umstadt, only noticing this after my GPS started beeping "off course!" at me. I stopped as quickly as I could, did a u-turn and pedalled back uphill to my route.

My downhill fun returned, but then I was bleeped at and told to turn off the main road, which I did. For some reason that I don't understand, but can only put down to some kind of mapping glitch, I spent the next mile or so riding through a rough track in a field, before returning to exactly the same road I'd left only moments before.

I'd very much returned to "civilization" now – the towns were bigger and more modern, the distances between them were less and the roads were much busier. I was still sticking mostly to bike paths and minor roads, but every now and then I had to cross a major road which was sometimes a bit frantic. I was always glad to see a bike path to take refuge from the traffic. This last part of the day was always the worst. In the morning I was rested and had plenty of energy, but later in the day I was tired and if I was going to make mistakes, it was going to be now. I found myself on a not particularly bike-friendly road that ran alongside the A26 Autobahn. It was pretty busy, but there was no bike path and had no shoulder. It was the correct road, but if I had been given an option, I wouldn't have ridden on it. I was grateful when the route departed from it at Gundernhausen, only to be disappointed again shortly afterwards when I returned to the same road. I needed a break, so I stopped at a petrol station to grab a drink.

As I emerged from the shop, I was greeted by a guy with a mountain bike. I was a little wary initially – he appeared a little eccentric, but seemed genuine. He saw I was loaded up and asked me about my trip, which I duly explained. He asked where I was going and if he could ride with me for a while. I was still a bit on guard, but I didn't see what harm it could do. He also said that he knew a good route in to Darmstadt, which I found quite appealing given my recent experience with the main road. I finished my drink and went to throw the bottle in the bin, but he stopped me and asked if he could have the bottle as it had a deposit. I had no problem with this, to he stuck it in his bag and off we rode.

Truth be told, his route was undoubtedly much better than mine, as we tracked across fields on bike paths, then down an old railway track and through a forest, whereas my route continued down the main road most of the way. I had trouble keeping up with him sometimes, with my heavily laden bike and over 100 miles in my legs. We emerged from the forest in to the grounds of Darmstadt University campus, through which he skilfully navigated. We then went through the oldest remaining part of town, which I just wouldn't have seen had I not had my impromptu guide. Darmstadt was heavily bombed during World War II and the centre was almost entirely destroyed.

Eventually my guide and I parted ways, as he headed for his home and I my hotel. He gave me instructions on how I should get to my hotel, but after he had left I reverted to Google Maps. It was gone 6pm now and while not dark, the light was very patchy in the tree-lined avenues, so I turned on my flashing rear light. Just minutes later, I was hailed by a German driver, who wound down his window to talk to me. After some initial confusion with the language, it turned out that he was asking me about my rear light – which as it turns out is illegal in Germany, although he admitted it was very effective!

Shortly after I had arrived in the centre of the city, or at least as close to the centre as I was going to get. It had been another long day and all I wanted to do was shower and get something to eat. I found my hotel pretty easily, checked in and took my bike down to the garage where I locked it up. I grabbed my bags and went up to my room in the lift, where I promptly dropped all my bags and drank both bottles of complementary water. I guess I must have been thirsty. I had a quick shower and changed ready to find something to eat. Google had lots of suggestions for places I could eat, but as I walked up the road the options within walking distance appeared to be a kebab house or a Mexican restaurant. I chose the latter. After munching down a plate of nachos, a chimichanga and a couple of beers I was done for the day. I headed back to the hotel, updated Facebook and my blog, called Jill and fell asleep in front of the television.

*Descending in to Herrenzimmern, Germany*

# DAY 12 – DARMSTADT TO BOPPARD

108 miles.

I woke in the middle of the night feeling a little unwell – hot, sweaty and nauseous. I was concerned I might have eaten something bad. Perhaps the chimichanga had disagreed with me? I propped myself up in bed a little and felt a little better after a while, but for a moment I even considered booking another night in the hotel and having a rest day. I must have fallen asleep again, as when I woke later I felt significantly better.

Breakfast was included at the hotel in Darmstadt, so I had a lie-in until 6am before heading downstairs at 6.30 for my buffet breakfast. After having my fill, I returned to my room, grabbed my gear and headed down to the garage for my bike. It was still there. I attached my bags, walked up the ramp and fired up my GPS.

Yesterday's route wasn't supposed to end in Darmstadt; the original route had ended near Mainz, but the recalculated route finished in Darmstadt as I had planned to perhaps meet up with an ex-colleague who lived here. Anyway, the planned "Day 12" route was Mainz to Koblenz, not Darmstadt to Koblenz. However, every time I load a route on my GPS, it offers "Would you like to navigate to the start of the course?", a function which I never use, because usually I am near the start of the course. On this occasion, I answered "yes", take me to the start of the course. Near Mainz. What could possibly go wrong?

I headed out of Darmstadt with the confidence of a man who knew where he was going, which of course, I didn't. All I had was a 2.6" LCD screen which showed a tiny map of my immediate surroundings and how far it was to the next turn. I was blissfully unaware that I was heading south, not north-west. All I knew was that I had about 30 miles to go before I arrived in Mainz. Meanwhile, hundreds of miles away, back in England, people were wondering (well, Captain Ann was anyway), why I was heading in completely the wrong direction.

Some explanation is probably required here, because I haven't mentioned it up until now; after the trip to Immingham and back revealed a major flaw in my tracking system (an app on my phone which drained the battery quicker than you can say "GPS"), I'd invested in a state-of-the art tracking device. OK, so it was a dog tracker, but it worked pretty well. I'd published a link which allowed everyone following my trip on social media to track my location across Europe in real-time. I had joked in some of my vlogs (video blogs) that at times I had no clue where I was and that people following my tracker probably had a better idea of where I was than I did. On this occasion that statement was 100% true.

I seemed to be progressing well, riding steadily down a selection of bike paths and back roads, mostly incorrectly following the Bundesstraße 3 in a southerly direction. At Lorsch I turned west – still the wrong direction, but slightly less wrong, perhaps. Progress was still good, until I arrived at Bürstadt, where the main road was blocked due to resurfacing works. I diverted around these and continued on the road, but a little further on there was another road block – it seemed like the bridge over the highway was closed. I pulled up Google Maps on my phone (amazingly I still hadn't twigged that I was off course) and re-routed around the road block via some back roads and rough bike paths.

The first inkling I had that all was not well, was when I crossed the river Rhine at Worms. I wasn't expecting to cross the Rhine at Worms. I was expecting to cross it at Mainz. I carried on a little further until I spotted a cafe in the *Marktplatz* square that I thought would be a good place to stop for elevenses. I ordered myself a large coffee and a selection of kuchen and went and sat in the sun to eat. That's when I pulled out my phone and zoomed out on Google Maps to see where exactly I was.

What!? I thought. Instead of riding 35km north-west, I'd ridden 46km south-west and I was now still 50km away from where I should have been! Thanks Garmin! I was just a little bit annoyed. I was also resigned to the fact that there was nothing I could do about it now. It would take me another 2 ½ hours to get to Mainz, meaning that I would have taken 5 ½ hours to get there instead of the 1 ½ that it should have. I finished my coffee, sat in the *Marktplatz* and made a quick video update for Facebook. I then plotted a route from Worms to Mainz and uploaded it to my GPS. There was no way I was going to trust it to navigate any further – who knows where I might end up?

On the bright side, I had at least visited Worms, which despite being heavily bombed in World War II did still have some very attractive buildings, including St. Peter's cathedral and the Nibelungentower on the bridge over the Rhine. I headed south out of Worms on the bike path nest to the *Landesstraße* 439 regional road, which was pretty quiet all the same. On my left was a range of low hills, entirely covered with vineyards, while to my right was the flat floodplain of the Rhine valley. I passed through a few small towns, all of which seemed to have at least one winery with signs outside offering wine tasting and sales. I was definitely tempted, but resisted in favour of a cold drink and an ice-cream at Guntersblum.

I'd been cutting off a curve in the river Rhine, but returned to it just after Oppenheim. I rode alongside the B9 *Bundesstraße*, on a bike path, but at some stage I missed a turning, because the bike path vanished and I found myself riding along a busy road between a railway and the Rhine, with no option but to continue. If I'd only known what *Achtung radfahrer! Letzte möglichkeit zum radweg Nackenheim-Mainz* (Attention cyclists! Last possibility to the Nackenheim-Mainz cycle path.) had meant at the time, I could have been riding through a vineyard on the EuroVelo 15 instead. I think this was the only time I was actually tooted by a German motorist, probably more to say "why are you on the main road you crazy man?" than out of annoyance. I can only say that nobody was keener to get off the road than I. Unfortunately the opportunity wouldn't arise until 3 or 4 miles later, but as soon as it did, I took it.

I'd accidentally found one of the branches of the EV15 now, which was to take me all the way to my ferry at Hook of Holland and after a few more miles, I arrived in Mainz, at the confluence of the rivers Main and Rhine. This was where my original route for the day had started and where I had hoped to be several hours ago. I cancelled my hastily-calculated route (which I had named "Grrr!") and loaded "12 – Mainz to Koblenz", although there was zero chance of me actually getting to Koblenz now as it was 90 miles away and it was already 1pm.

Only minutes in to my new route I ran in to another problem! The EV15 ran down a spit of land between the Mainz yacht club and the Rhine, then crossed over a swing bridge back to the riverside, only the swing bridge was closed. A few cyclists had done the same thing and we were all waiting to see if this was a temporary closure, or something more long-term. It appeared that the work might have been completed, as the bridge did start to move back, but shortly afterwards it stopped again. There was nothing to do but back-track around the yacht club again. OK, so it wasn't a long diversion, but bothersome nonetheless.

Shortly later, I did something that I'd sworn I wasn't going to do on this trip. As I was leaving Mainz, I spotted a Burger King and I succumbed. It was nearly 2pm, 28°C, I was hot, tired and hungry…

The next 15 miles were a bit odd. The EV15 weaved through an industrial estate, then through what I can only describe as a load of allotments, before returning to the Rhine for a short while, then another industrial estate and more allotments. Finally, I rode along a raised levee for several miles, before finally returning to the river at Kempten am Rhein. I did sometimes wonder if my route was following the EV15, but there weren't any signs to say otherwise, so I have to assume it was.

Just after Kempton I stopped at a boat ramp to take a photo of the river and the steeply-pitched vineyards on the far bank. There was a young lady with a bike doing the same thing and she asked me if I wouldn't mind taking her photograph. With photos taken, we both rode off along the bike path together. It transpired that she was Dutch and riding from Switzerland, home to the Netherlands. She was fairly lightly-loaded and covering about 100km a day on her gravel bike. She was also riding a lot faster than I was, so after a few miles I made the excuse of stopping to take another photo and she rode off in to the distance.

The route now stuck to the side of the Rhine, which at this point was flowing between steep hills on either side of the valley. To the west, there were forests and to the east, vineyards, interspersed with pretty villages with white-painted walls. There were plenty of boats plying the route up and down the river, big white river cruisers with large picture windows and commercial traffic too. The flow of the river here must have been fairly fast, because the barges working their way upstream were making much harder work than those heading downstream. There were railways on both sides of the river too and every now and then a passenger train, or a huge freight train would pass by. Occasionally the railways disappeared in to tunnels, only to reappear a short while later. They had certainly managed to squeeze as much infrastructure as possible between the river and the hillside. At each bend in the river there seemed to be another fairytale castle, some in ruins, some that have been repurposed in to hotels. Since 2002, the Rhine Gorge has been a UNESCO world heritage site because of its beauty as a cultural landscape.

I wound my way further and further down the Rhine, through small towns and villages, all of which might have had places to stay because I was most definitely on the tourist trail. Time was marching on though and I wasn't going to make Koblenz before nightfall, that was certain, so I stopped for a few minutes to see where I might stay that evening and after a little deliberation found a hotel in the town of Boppard, about an hour further down the river. I rode the bike path all the way down by the side of the river and just after 6pm rolled up outside my stop for the night.

The hotel was obviously popular with bikers (of the motorized kind) as when I arrived there were a row of UK registered motorbikes outside, although I didn't see any of the riders while I was there. I checked in and asked where I might store my bicycle and was given directions to the cycle garage down to one side. In the garage in the basement were a number of bicycles, mostly e-bikes and I had to duck under a number of cables as the majority were on charge. I locked my bike and took the lift to my room with a view, overlooking the road and the railway. I'm sure if I had paid more I could have had one overlooking the river, but given that I would be mostly asleep I didn't think it was very good value for money.

Showered and changed I popped down to the river's edge to make a quick evening video update, making a hasty retreat as soon as I was done as I was being attacked by mosquitoes. I returned to the hotel and had a look at the options for dinner, which were few. Either I could stay in the hotel and have the buffet, or I could walk 20 minutes to the town centre. Unsurprisingly, I opted to stay in the hotel. The buffet was OK and reasonable priced anyway, so I couldn't complain. There was no bar, but there was a vending machine that had soft drinks, snacks and beer, so I purchased a bottle and retired to my room to drown my sorrows. I was still annoyed at the morning's navigational issues and I would definitely made Koblenz if I hadn't of had them, possibly even Bonn. That would all have to wait for tomorrow now.

*Burg Pfalzgrafenstein, Kaub, Germany*

# Day 13 – Boppard to Dormagen

104 miles.

Before today I'd never heard of either of these places, but that's part of the adventure. I had a few passes at the breakfast buffet this morning before heading down to the bicycle garage to head off. Even more e-bikes on charge this morning, but once I'd untangled myself from them all I was on the road at 7.45am. Today, as yesterday I would be continuing down the EuroVelo 15 Rhine cycle path, which meant that at least the route would be flat. I was through Boppard in no time at all and soon arrived in the town of Spay. I stopped to take a photograph of the imposing 12th century Marksburg castle on the opposite bank of the river. Curiously, Marksburg castle has an exact replica, built in the Ueno German Cultural Village on the Southern island of Miyakojima, Japan, which was built after the owner of the original castle refused to have it demolished and rebuilt in Japan.

After about an hour on the road I was arriving at the outskirts of Koblenz. It was just as well I didn't try and reach the city last night, as almost immediately I arrived I ran in to issues. Not huge ones, just minor diversions, but in the dark I'm sure they would have been harder to negotiate. The bike path next to the river was closed, forcing me to back-track and pick another route through the streets. To be fair, there were diversion signs especially in place for the bike path, which were not too hard to follow. I returned to the bike path once more, only to find it closed again shortly later with a huge pile-driver parked in it. This time the diversion was less obvious and more complicated and I found myself winding through the centre of the city before crossing the river Moselle on the Balduinbrücke (Baldwin Bridge). From the bridge I had an excellent view of the imposing Ehrenbreitstein Fortress, built by the Prussians between1817 and 1828. With a photograph duly taken, I doubled back to the banks of the Rhine and continued through a camping and caravan park, which was still very busy. The EV15 then took a detour around the Koblenz Rhine Port, an inland container port. I was pretty much through Koblenz now, although this part of the Rhine was so built up and industrial it was difficult to tell where one town ended and another started.

I was still riding down the river bank, with the Rhine to my right and some obviously desirable riverside properties to my left. Ironically, just after passing some of these, I also passed the Mülheim-Kärlich Nuclear Power Plant. I wouldn't actually have known this, had I not been forced yet again to back-track and divert from the bike path due to more roadworks. The plant itself is inactive and although it only came online in 1986, it only operated for three years before being taken out of action. Legal problems repeatedly prevented it being brought back online and the decommissioning process was started in 2001.

Shortly later I stopped in Weißenthurm in a park by the river and had a banana and some chocolate. I'd been riding for a couple of hours and had done my 25 miles. I made a quick morning update video for Facebook before moving on. A coffee would have been nice, but although there were a few restaurants, none appeared to be open yet. Just around the bend from Weißenthurm I had to detour around the Andernach Rhine Port the largest container port on the middle Rhine. In contrast to the huge port, the town itself, especially the old town, is tiny.

Just after Andernach, the infrastructure engineers had surpassed themselves, as between the steep hill side and the banks of the Rhine, they have managed to squeeze in two roads, a railway and a bicycle path. They have achieved this by building the *Bundesstraße*, B19 on an elevated section, with the bike path and the railway running underneath it at times, and the *Landesstraße* L117 alongside the river. All this in the space of about 70 metres (300 feet). This marvel or modern engineering continued for a while, before the valley widened out slightly allowing for more conventional construction. This didn't last long though before the next squeeze, although not quite as tight as the last one. This continued until the valley widened, at least for a while, at Remagen.

The name Remagen is mostly associated with the 1969 film, The Bridge at Remagen, based on the book of the same name. While the film has taken a lot of artistic license there is some truth behind the story. The Ludendorff Bridge (at Remagen) was one of the few remaining bridges over the Rhine left intact, captured by the 9th Armoured Division of the US Army. The German defenders had wired it with over two tons of explosives, but some failed on detonation, leaving the bridge largely intact. US forces captured the bridge and used it much to their advantage to establish a bridgehead on the far side. The Germans repeatedly attempted to destroy it but it was successfully defended until it finally collapsed 10 days after it was captured. The bridge was never rebuilt and all that remains is a museum incorporated in to the piers at one end and a performing arts space at the other.

After Remagen, the squeeze begins again, continuing for the next 5 or 6 miles, almost until Bonn. On the left bank of the river now are the Eifel uplands on the left the Siebengebirge hills, dotted with the last castles of the Rhine valley, Schloss Drachenburg and Löwenburg, almost like a last gasp before the North German Plain. Eventually the valley started to open out south of Bonn and at the Mehlem-Königswinter ferry jetty I spotted an open kiosk serving food. It had only just gone midday, but I'd ridden just over 50 miles so decided to stop for a break. It was pretty warm too – not the 30-plus degrees I'd experienced in the Hungarian plains, but high twenties.

I opted for a Currywurst and fries, plus a cold drink. I sat on my plastic chair at my plastic table and munched away, under the persistent gaze of a spaniel that was trying to hypnotize me in to sharing some of my food. His owners pulled him back, but he wasn't giving up that easily. I explained that I had three dogs at home and it didn't bother me, I was used to it. Currywurst is a peculiarly German invention and is nothing more than a Bratwurst sausage in a tomato/curry sauce, sprinkled with curry powder, allegedly invented post-WW2 by a lady called Herta Heuwer in West Berlin, who obtained ketchup and curry powder from British soldiers in Germany.

I finished my meal without spaniel intervention and continued my journey north towards Bonn. The bike path continued alongside the river, but to my left now were the leafy suburbs of the city. These briefly gave way to the Freizeitpark Rheinaue, a large park, before I arrived at the United Nations Campus and the site of the Bonn Bundeshaus, seat of the German Government from 1949 until 1999. Although East and West Germany were reunified in 1990, there was some discussion on where the seat of government should be and this wasn't settled until 1991 when the government voted by a narrow margin to move this back to Berlin.

I crossed the Rhine at the Friedrich-Ebert bridge, which carries the Autobahn over the river north of Bonn, but fortunately also has a convenient cycle-lane. The approaches make the bridge over 1km long and there was an impressive spiral bike-path on the left bank that took me through a 360° loop rising to the bridge deck. On the right bank the bike path is less complicated, but confused my GPS for a while as it looped back on itself, then under the bridge before connecting to the L269 highway. I was then taken through the Siegaue nature reserve and eventually back to the banks of the Rhine.

Luxury homes lined this tide of the river, build high on the banks, behind high walls in case of flooding, or behind a defensive levee that also carried the bike path. This side of the river was slightly less populated than the other, but it was still frequently punctuated with towns and villages. The route stuck largely to the riverside though and I was able to zip along nicely, edging closer and closer to the next large city, Cologne. At 3pm it was time for another break, so I stopped at a cafe next to the Campingplatz Stadt Köln, the city campsite. I felt like it was too late for lunch, but too early for dinner, so I settled for a coffee and an apple strudel with ice-cream. That would keep me going for a while, at least. I'd ridden 78 miles and for 7 hours now. I wasn't sure where I was aiming for today – my GPS route ended in Duisberg, but that would have made for a 140 mile day. I was still playing catch-up from my impromptu diversion to Worms!

A few miles further and I crossed back to the left bank again, over the Deutzer bridge in Cologne. Oddly enough this was familiar ground, as I'd only recently been here in July with Jill, as part of our InterRail trip. I reappeared on the river bank near the Lindt Chocolate Museum – which I can highly recommend, although I didn't visit this time. I rode quickly along the banks of the river, which I'd only walked along a couple of months ago, past the jetties with river cruisers moored up against them, stopping only to take a picture of Cologne cathedral, which miraculously survived the terrible bombing raid of 1942 mainly due to it being used as a point of reference by the allied bombers. I carried on down the river, past a container terminal and duly arrived at the Ford motor factory. This is a massive, 256 hectare site, which since 1929 has been the German factory HQ. It seemed like it was taking forever to pass, but in reality it was only 10 minutes. I still counted three tram stations outside the factory though, which should give you an idea of the size of the plant.

Just after the Ford plant I was forces to make a diversion yet again, as the bike path was closed as it passed under the A1 Autobahn. It wasn't too tricky this time though and I was soon back on track. Almost immediately, on the other side of the Autobahn I was back out in the countryside again – at least for a while. I rode along a levee, with fields on either side, then through a couple of small riverside villages which looked very much like they might have been regularly flooded, judging by the high walls and flood gates.

A little further on, I started to feel the splash of rain. It had been threatening for a while, with big black clouds to the north, the direction in which I was headed. I stopped beneath a gantry over the road that carried pipes from one of the jetties by the river in to a massive chemical park to my left, it didn't offer much protection, but it was better than nothing. It wasn't raining that heavily, but it didn't look like it was going to get any better, so I pulled on my waterproof shoe covers and my rain cape. I carried on down the levee for another half an hour, the rain getting steadily heavier and heavier. At the medieval town of Zons I thought enough was enough and called it a day. Shortly afterwards I was due to cross the river on the Zons-Urdenbach ferry, but there was nowhere to shelter and I was getting soaked. I'd done my 100 miles anyway and after ten hours in the saddle I was ready for a rest.

I coasted down towards Zons and tried to find somewhere under cover where I might be able to use my phone to find a hotel. This was harder than anticipated, but eventually I found a tree that might suffice. It didn't help much though, as water kept dripping on to my phone, making almost impossible to use. It quickly became obvious that Zons itself wasn't going to be an option, as there was only one "Hotel Schloss Friedestrom" and it was out of my price range. I expanded my search a little further and picked the "Top Hotel Garni" in Dormagen, which looked like the best option available. It was 15 minutes ride away, but it would have to do.

I set it as a destination on Google Maps and threw my phone in my handlebar bag. I had to keep flipping open the lid so I could see where I was going because I couldn't hear the audio prompts above the rain. In due course I arrived at "Top Hotel Garni", but it didn't look particularly "Top" to me. In fact, it looked closed. Closer inspection revealed a letter in the window, in German, obviously. I attempted to decipher it and eventually with the help of my translation app I discovered that it had been taken over by the Hotel Ragusa and I should go there, which I duly did.

Fortunately the hotel Ragusa was only a couple of minutes away. I arrived at the hotel, which looked a lot more open, dumped my bike outside and went to reception. I explained that I had booked and paid for a room at "Top Hotel Garni" on my hotel app and it looked for a moment that I was going to end up as the only resident in the "Top Hotel Garni" but they decided to put me up in the Ragusa instead, which to me looked like an upgrade and I was happy to accept. I was shown to my room, then shown where I might put my bike under cover for the night and everything was looking good.

By the time I had showered and changed, it was past 7pm and time for dinner. I looked on my phone, but it seemed like the hotel Ragusa was the most happening place in Dormagen, which doesn't say much. I strolled out in to the square to make a video for social media (it had stopped raining now) and wandered down to the main street, but even on a Friday night it all seemed pretty quiet. The only highlight for me was a shop selling some amazing looking lighting fixtures. Back at the Ragusa I ordered dinner and I must say it was very good and the staff were very attentive.

Back in my room, I did my usual Facebook update and blog post, then made a quick call to Jill. That done, I was off to bed, hoping for dry weather in the morning.

*Remagen*

# Day 14 – Dormagen to Wageningen

116 miles.

Up bright and early again this morning and ready for breakfast as soon as it was available. I think I heard someone working away in the kitchen at 5am, so true dedication from the chef on a Saturday morning. I munched away on my buffet breakfast, returned to my room and got everything ready, then went out and retrieved my bike and I was underway just past 7am.

Cooler again this morning, although nowhere near as cold as it had been in Bavaria, but still dark as I headed out of Dormagen on the B9 towards Düsseldorf. I didn't head back to Zons and the ferry, because I had no idea what time it started running and made a beeline for the city instead. I rode along the bike path next to the road and after about 20 minutes I picked up the river again. The sun was just rising and there was shallow fog over the Rhine, which looked lovely in the morning sun, so I stopped to take a couple of photos. I was heading for the Fleher Bridge, taking the A45 Autobahn in to the south of the city. Again, I stopped half way across to take a photo of the concrete tower supporting the main span. At the other end of the bridge I passed through some woods on a bike path and reappeared in a park, just where the Autobahn disappears into a tunnel under the city. Here I picked up my original route again, which actually followed the EuroVelo 4 "Central Europe Route" right through the city centre, until it linked up with the EV15 on the other side.

I was a bit apprehensive about this part of the route as riding through any city with a population of over 600,000 might be fraught with potential hazards, but it transpired that the cycle paths were very good, plus the fact that I was there at 8 am on a Saturday morning made for a quiet ride through what I thought was a pleasant city. I stopped to take a couple of photos and probably should have taken more. Sounds like I might have to go back! I rejoined the Rhine near the concert hall and rode through the Rheinpark Golzheim, a riverside park with large open areas that seemed popular with runners.

The EV15 continued along a low levee, which was clearly underneath the flight path of Düsseldorf airport on the north side of town. A couple of miles after the airport I cut inland a little, across a bend in the river and past a patchwork of fields. It wasn't long before I was approaching Duisberg, the next large city on my agenda. Yet again I zig-zagged through the suburbs along bike paths and down leafy streets and I soon found myself in the city centre. I stopped in a cafe for a coffee and kuchen for my 3 hour/30 mile break and made a quick video update for my followers on social media.

Now, I knew I had a couple of bridges to cross in Duisberg, the first over the Ruhr and the second, back over the Rhine again. While I was sitting in the cafe I noticed on Google Maps that the first bridge seemed to be closed. The second bridge was open, but if I couldn't get to it, that was kind of irrelevant. The other problem was that the next closest bridge also seemed to be closed, which meant I might be in for a sizeable detour. I asked the waiter if he knew whether the Ruhr bridge was closed to bikes or not, but he just replied "Keine Ahnung" (no idea) and that was that. I decided to chance the Ruhr bridge, as I knew that often "closed", doesn't necessarily mean "closed to bikes". A mile later I had my answer. On this occasion "closed" meant "closed". I decided to head for the Rhine bridge instead, to see how closed that was. I went to and fro for a while, trying to make my way to the downstream side of the bridge, where I thought I could see a bike path. After a couple of miles I found my way there and there was a bike path, furthermore, it was open. I could also now understand the "closed" status – a new bridge was being constructed alongside the old bridge.

I crossed the bridge and dropped back down to the riverside and continued on the EV15 on the river bank. I was almost back on track, when I arrived at the *rheinpreußenhafen* – the Rhine-Prussian port. Over the mouth of the port is a steel constructed lifting bridge, the Homberg lift bridge. Unfortunately this too was closed, awaiting renovation by the city. I pulled out my phone and looked at my GPS route, comparing it to Google and decided the easiest thing to do was to ignore the GPS and head straight down the main road, cutting off the corner. My GPS would moan at me, but that couldn't be avoided. True to form, as I rode down the main road on the shoulder, my GPS beeped at me continuously, telling me I was off course, turn left, turn right, make a u-turn, until a couple of miles later it decided that the best way to return to the route was to go the way I was already going. Eventually it found the course and shut up, at least for a while.

For the next 10 miles things went pretty smoothly. I followed the Rhine for a while, then cut across a couple of S bends in the river through some small towns and villages. I stopped to buy something to eat later in Orsoy before quickly moving on through the next town, Rheinburg. These towns seemed generally fairly modern, while they might have had a older centre square, they were a lot less picturesque to ride through now than just about everything else up to now.

My good fortune didn't continue though, as just after Ossenberg the EV15 took a right turn and continued along a levee, but right at the turning was a barrier and signs indicating that section was closed. I was expecting this, to be honest, as I'd been closely following the EuroVelo discussion group online and somebody had mentioned that there were a number of closures between Duisberg and Hook of Holland. I checked my maps and decided that I should just be able to skirt around this section by staying on the main roads (well, the bike-paths alongside them), so that's exactly what I did.

I rejoined my route at the town of Büderich, which didn't seem anything special, but as I exited the town I saw a little monument on my left. There was also a bench, so I thought it might be a good place for lunch. As I had my little picnic I read some of the display signs. It seems that Büderich was established in 1138, but not the town I'd just ridden through, rather here, 1.5km down the road. It managed to survive for several centuries, before it was razed to the ground in 1813 by Napoleonic troops retreating from the Russian campaign of 1812. The new town was rebuilt in its current location from 1815 and despite being flooded a number of times has survived up until now.

After lunch and my impromptu history lesson I carried on down the road, before turning back on to the EV15 and continuing along a levee by the Rhine. There were a few villages to the left of me protected from flooding by the levee, but it seemed like a precarious location all the same. I skirted to the east of Xanten, which for some reason I thought was in the Netherlands, not Germany. I'm not sure why, but probably because it begins with an "X". That's undoubtedly not a very good reason, but it is the only place in Germany that does begin with an "X". I was psychologically prepared to leave Germany today and enter the Netherlands, but Germany seemed to be going on forever! I rode past Xantener Sudsee, a lake just north of Xanten, then got a little lost in the town or Wardt due to a road closure. I was looking at my phone when a couple came zipping past me on e-bikes, looking as if they knew where they were going, so I decided to follow them. Luckily they were heading in the same direction as me, because after a few turns I was back on EV15, riding along the side of Xantener Nordsee.

Half an hour later I was confronted with a more serious looking closure. On the other side of the Rhine from Emmerich the entire road was closed to traffic, not just the bike path. This was a bit of a problem, as the EV15 continued on the left bank of the Rhine for another 20 miles before it crossed the river. I could weave around a few local roadworks, but these weren't local – they were going to put me miles off course. Unfortunately there was nothing for it. I cancelled the route on my GPS to stop the constant bleeping and headed over the suspension bridge to Emmerich. I stopped on the other side of the river and pulled up my routing app to plot a route from where I was, to link up with where my original route resumed, just outside Arnhem. The resulting route turned out to be remarkably simple – it just followed the B8 to the border, then the same road in the Netherlands.

After a bit of a false start riding up the wrong side of the B8 on a bike path to nowhere, I back-tracked and crossed to the bike path on the correct side and got on pretty well. I zipped through the last couple of villages in Germany, Hüthum and Elten and a couple of miles further up the road I crossed a speed hump in to the Netherlands.

*Bridge from Uedesheim to Düsseldorf, Germany*

# Chapter 12. The Netherlands

It had seemed like a long time coming, but I had finally arrived in the Netherlands. Not that there was anything wrong with Germany – I had very much appreciated the excellent cycling infrastructure and the polite and patient drivers, but arriving in the Netherlands felt like progress.  Of course the Netherlands is renowned for it's bike paths and I was expecting good things. I wasn't disappointed. There were bike paths alongside all of the roads and where they met with junctions and roundabouts there were dashed white lines crossing them, with cyclists having right of way.

In the Netherlands, cyclists are protected by a strict liability law. The car is deemed responsible in any collision between a cyclist and a car, regardless of fault. This means that cars, when approaching a junction must allow cyclists to pass. It was a bit odd to start with, as I was approaching junctions as I would in the UK, slowing or stopping as I got to them. This resulted in drivers looking at me oddly, probably thinking "there goes another crazy Englishman…" Soon, however, I got used to the fact that drivers would stop and I made like the locals, flying across the junctions without a second thought!

I made great progress and within the hour I was at the outskirts of Arnhem. I stopped then to see if I could find somewhere to stay for the night. I opened my app, but it didn't look good. It was the same situation as last night, only without the rain. Everywhere in Arnhem was booked up, or too expensive. Jill always complains when I leave everything until the last possible minute and prefers to have everything booked weeks in advance. That just wasn't possible on this trip as on many occasions I had no clue where I might finish the day. That's why I usually pulled up by the roadside and looked for somewhere about an hour away or so. It was a shame, because I'd have liked to have arrived early in Arnhem to have a look around.

I expanded my search radius and found somewhere in Wageningen that met with my requirements, about 15 miles away. Not ideal, but it would have to do. I plotted a route with my app, uploaded it to the GPS and soon I was underway. It didn't take long before I was in Arnhem city centre. I didn't stop, but my first impressions were of a modern city and not entirely what I expected. Probably watched "A Bridge Too Far" too many times.

On the other side of Arnhem I was a little surprised to find my self riding up some hills – I thought the Netherlands was supposed to be flat? To be honest, they weren't big hills, but I was running out of energy.

It was gone 6pm and I'd been riding since 7am this morning and hadn't really eaten properly all day. I still had nearly 10 miles to go, so stopped at a petrol station and did something I never did before – I bought a Mars bar and a Red Bull. I mean, I've eaten Mars bars before, but not Red Bull. I needed something to give me an energy boost.

It seemed to work, because shortly later I was flying along at the giddy speed of 15 MPH, although that might have been because it was slightly downhill too. I left the main road after a while and headed down a bike path entering the south side of Wageningen, but not before riding along the river Nederrijn for a while and spotting my last Rhine cruiser, or should that be Nederrijn cruiser? I passed through the town centre and shortly later, I pulled up outside the hotel. I'd been on the road for 12 hours and ridden 116 difficult miles.

I locked my bike up outside, because there seemed to be a lot of people milling about, then went to check in. This is when I discovered that the people milling around were at a wedding reception being held at the hotel, which also meant that the restaurant was closed. Not good news. I asked about bike storage and was advised that there was a locked storage area and given some directions towards it. I mustn't have been listening, because I just couldn't find it outside. I retuned to reception and the young man replied that it wasn't outside at all, it was inside the hotel down a passage by reception.

With my bike safely stored away, I went to my room and flopped down in a chair. After a few minutes to compose myself, I made a quick video update for Facebook. That done, I dealt with dinner by means of ordering a pizza before taking a shower. Showered and changed, I sat and watched Dutch TV for a while before dinner arrived. Dinner was a bit of an anticlimax after such an eventful day, but that was probably just as well. Even though I was hungry I struggled to eat as I was so tired. After a while I gave up, collapsed on the bed and fell asleep.

# DAY 15 – WAGENINGEN TO ROTTERDAM

62 miles.

I think I was the first person in the breakfast hall again today – this was beginning to be habit forming! I wasn't particularly early, because looking at my route I only had about 90 miles to get to Hook of Holland and my ferry didn't leave until 10pm, so I had plenty of time.

A few days ago I had resigned myself to the fact that I wasn't going to make my original sailing date (Saturday 30th), so I had changed my sailing date to Monday 2nd, which seemed like a more realistic target.

It now looked like today, the 1st October was the target, so I brought my departure forward again. I couldn't see how anything could scupper my plans now.

With all my kit packed away, I wheeled my bike out of the hotel and set off. After a couple of miles riding beside the road I diverted off to a bike path beside the Nederrijn again. I rode alongside the river, passing through small towns and villages. There were a few people out and about wearing their Sunday best, presumably on their way to church. I then followed the main road to Amerongen, where again I left the main road and followed the course of the river. I was riding along the top of a dyke, the *Lekdijk*, with the river to my left and fields to my right. It was bright and sunny, not too hot yet, but it was windy. Not that windy, but enough of a breeze to make itself felt and unfortunately I was heading straight in to it. The wind certainly wouldn't have qualified for the Dutch Headwind Cycling Championships, which is an annual event held on the Eastern Scheldt Storm Surge Barrier along the North Sea coast. For that event to take place the winds speed needs to be 32MPH or higher and competitors must ride the 8.5 km course against the wind on upright single-speed bicycles.

Further along the dyke, near Wijk bij Duurstede, I spotted my first windmill, the "Molen Rijn en Lek". It seemed to be a bit of a tourist attraction, as there were large crowds of people there too. The Nederrijn, the Lek and the Amsterdam Rijnkanall meet here and I crossed over the double locks here too. The Amsterdam–Rhine Canal joins Amsterdam to the Rhine, as its name suggests, passing through Utrecht on its way, carrying an average of 100,000 ships a year.

I continued westward, conveniently riding along in the slipstream of a couple of ladies on traditional Dutch bicycles for a while, until I felt like a bit of a cheat, so I overtook them and felt the force of the headwind for a while. I kept pushing hard in to the headwind, hoping to have distanced myself from them a little because I'd have felt a little foolish if I'd turned around and they were still there. Luckily, when I did chance a look behind, they were nowhere to be seen.

After 2 ½ hours I'd ridden 25 miles and rather conveniently a cafe appeared at Schalkwijk right at the correct moment. I sat outside in the sun and ordered a coffee and an apple strudel with some cream, which seemed like a good option. I sat and ate under the close scrutiny of a tabby cat, who made it clear that she too liked cream. After I had eaten I uploaded a quick video for Facebook and set off in to the headwind once more.

I carried on along through Nieuwegein and then followed the Benschopper Wetering canal for quite a long time through a succession of small villages. I knew I was getting closer and closer to Rotterdam and thought it would probably be a good place to stop for lunch, although time was marching on a bit. I felt a little hot and bothered, although I don't think it was that warm – mid 20's, maybe. I'd now clocked up 50 miles and not eaten much, but I just felt a bit weak and listless. I sent a message to the group chat:

*Me: I feel rubbish. Feel a bit sick. Don't know why. It's only 25 miles to Hook. I need to find somewhere to rest a bit*

I stopped on a bench by the side of the bike path for a bit of a rest. I had some drink from my bidon and a little bit of chocolate and rested for a few minutes.

Just as I set off again, I was passed by a young lady on roller blades. I set off in pursuit, but try as I might, I couldn't catch up with her. I didn't have it in me. I arrived in one of the suburbs of Rotterdam - Krimpen aan den IJssel to be precise, and spotted a petrol station. I thought perhaps maybe I was dehydrated, so I bought a fizzy drink there and sat outside an drank it all.

I carried on and my GPS bleeped at me, suggesting I had to cross the *Algerabrug*, a bridge over the river IJssel. Initially I wasn't sure how I was going to do that, as it looked as if I would have to carry my bike up two flights of steps. I was contemplating removing my panniers and shuttling them up individually, when another cyclist appeared and ran their front wheel up a ramp on one side of the steps. As soon as they did that, a small conveyor belt sprung in to action and pulled their bike up the ramp, while they climbed the steps alongside. Aha! I thought. I'll give that a try. It was a lot more difficult with a heavily loaded bike, but with a bit of a struggle, I was up at the bridge deck.

For some reason I then rode in the wrong direction, down the road, before my GPS started complaining at me. It was no good. I wasn't in a good state at all. First and foremost, I needed to find a bathroom, so I did what I always do in such circumstances - pulled up Google Maps and looked for the closest MacDonalds. Fortunately, there was one about a mile away. It still took me about 15 minutes to get there though, as I took a couple of wrong turns in my fragile state. I arrived though and headed straight to the bathroom. Once that emergency was dealt with, I ordered a coke and an ice-cream to see if a bit of sugar would help. It didn't. I messaged the chat:

*Me: I obviously ate something that disagreed with me*

I sat in MacDonalds, slowly finished my drink and my ice-cream, but I just felt worse and worse.

*Me: I think I'll have to find a hotel*

I had a look at my hotel app and booked a room in the closest hotel. I didn't really care how many stars it was or how much it cost, I just needed to find somewhere to stop. It was only 3 miles or so away, so it didn't take me long to get there. I checked in at the reception, explaining my predicament to the young lady at the reception. Once that was done, I asked if there was somewhere I could put my bike and she said I could store it in one of the conference rooms that wasn't in use. I went out to get my bike, while she helpfully held the door open for me, but I wasn't even half way to the door when I felt even worse. I rushed in to the toilets by reception, ran to a cubicle and was violently sick. When I thought I was done being sick, I cleaned up after myself as best I could and returned to the bemused lady in reception. This time we managed to get my bike in to the conference room. I grabbed my panniers and went to my room, which was fortunately on the ground floor. I let myself in and collapsed on the bed. Moments later I was in the bathroom projectile vomiting again. Afterwards, I had a small glass of water, then immediately brought it back up again. I was in a bad way. I sat on the floor in the bathroom for a while, just in case more incidents were forthcoming, then I went back and lay on the bed again, taking a plastic bin with me, just in case. Somehow I managed to change my ferry booking – there was no way I was going to get there today.

I must have fallen asleep, as the next think I knew was that I was awoken by a knock at my hotel door. It was the young lady from reception. Jill had read my messages in the group chat and used my dog tracker to locate where I was. She'd then called the hotel and asked them to check up on me. I assured the young lady that I didn't think I was going to expire, but I thought that I'd possibly got food poisoning or similar. She asked if I needed a doctor and I said I didn't think I did, but would it be possible if I could have a Coke? She disappeared and returned shortly afterwards with a small bottle. I knew I had to rehydrate, so I started taking small sips of Coke or hydration mix from my bidons, which seemed to stay down. This continued for the next few hours; I'd fall asleep, wake up, sip a little fluid and fall asleep again. I think it was about 2am when I managed to drink a small glass of water and not be immediately sick again, so things were improving.

*Vlist, Netherlands*

# Day 16 – Rotterdam to Hoek

25 miles.

In the morning, I got up and went to the reception to ask where I might buy something to eat. The lady there said that I could have breakfast and showed me where. The breakfast buffet was full of things that I would have loved to eat, like eggs, bacon, Danish pastries and suchlike, but I just couldn't face it. I asked if there was a supermarket nearby and she gave me directions. Walking to the supermarket probably helped me recover a little, a bit of fresh air. I bought some bananas and some crackers, that would have to do. Returning to the hotel, I verified the check-out time – it was 12 o'clock, so I went back to my room and stayed there, sipping water and eating crackers.

I left it to the absolute last minute to leave the hotel – I still felt rubbish, but it was only 25 miles, surely I could manage that? I packed up my panniers and went to the reception to check out. I recovered my bike from the conference room and set it up outside, hung on my panniers, turned on my GPS and pressed go. I retraced my steps back to MacDonalds and picked up yesterday's route, which took me along a bike path on a quiet street with a weed-covered rhyne on one side. For those of you not from Somerset, a rhyne (pronounced "reen") is a drainage ditch, used to drain marshy areas (like the Somerset levels) and turn them in to agricultural land. The road led through a residential area, with houses and low-rise apartment blocks for a while, before becoming more commercial, then finally I passed through the city centre, all on the excellent bike paths. Occasionally I passed over small canals, then eventually the Delfshavense Schie, the main shipping canal. The canals all lead to the river Nieuwe Maas, which are lined with harbours and freight terminals. These make up the eastern part of the Port of Rotterdam, the largest sea port in Europe and indeed the largest in the world, outside of East Asia. The south side of the river, all the way from Rotterdam to the North Sea is almost entirely made up of port facilities, whereas the north side is less so, but still hosts an enormous agricultural industry of greenhouses.

As I progressed further and further towards Hook of Holland, the buildings thinned out, although they never disappeared completely, beside the bike path that ran all the way to Hook of Holland, until eventually I appeared on a path alongside the river. This ran all the way to the ferry terminal, six or seven miles distant. I kept pace with a freighter that was also heading out along the river, although to be honest I think he was gaining on me!

In due course, I arrived at the ferry terminal. It had taken me three hours to ride 25 miles, about an hour longer than it would normally take me to cover such a distance. I rode in to the terminal to check out the facilities and soon figured out that basically, there were none. I rode out of the terminal again and along the bike path towards the town of Hoek van Holland, where I found a convenient bench and sat down to contemplate my options. I was ridiculously early. The ferry didn't leave for another seven hours or so, so I had time to kill.

I still felt pretty rough, but although it was past lunchtime, I didn't feel like eating much, although I did manage a banana. I lay down on the bench in the sunshine and fell asleep. I'm not sure how long I slept for, but I felt pretty toasted when I woke up. I had forgotten to put any sun cream on and had caught the sun on my face. With several hours still to wait, I rolled in to town and around the square, before sitting down outside a cafe and ordering a coffee. I stayed there for a couple of hours and ordered a couple more drinks, before deciding to head back to the ferry terminal to see if there was any movement.

There were a couple of cars and motorhomes queued up now, but it was hardly what you'd describe as "busy". Nevertheless, I propped my bike up against a bench and sat down to wait some more. Time passed and another cyclist arrived, who introduced himself as "Nate" from Australia. He had taken time out from work and had been cycling through Europe for that ast three months, also following some EuroVelo routes as far south as Croatia. We talked for a while and discussed our trips, which helped the time pass.

Eventually there were signs of life at the check-in and the gates were opened. I grabbed my bike and pushed it forward to the kiosk, passport and tickets were checked and I walked through in to the terminal. Nate and I were waved through to the front of the short queue, where I snapped a quick picture of the ferry. Several tugs were rushing to and fro, hooking up articulated trailers and shuttling them on board. Finally, a crew member instructed us to ride over to the ramp and walk up the painted pedestrian footway. We were guided to an area in the bowels of the ferry set aside for bicycles, where there were rails and ropes for us to secure our bikes. I tied my bike up, unhooked my bags and headed for my cabin. After walking up what seemed like endless flights of stairs, I arrived at the correct deck and walked down a long corridor to my cabin. I pushed open the door, dumped everything on the floor and sat on my bunk. The tannoy periodically announced how there was "great value dining" in the restaurant, but I stuck with crackers and bananas. All I wanted to do was curl up in bed and that's just what I did.

Shortly later, the tannoy announced that we were underway. I was going home.

# Chapter 13. England

## Day 17 – Harwich to Luton

102 miles

I woke to the tune of "Don't Worry Be Happy" at an ungodly hour being played over the tannoy, followed by an invitation to come and take breakfast in the restaurant. I pondered my still fragile state and opted for a flapjack in my cabin instead, followed by a shower.

In due course, we were invited to vacate our cabins and head on down to the car deck, so I grabbed my bags, gave the cabin a cursory check to make sure I hadn't left anything and headed down. There were a lot more bicycles this morning than there were last night, including a tandem in the same bay as mine. The owners of the tandem were busy getting all their kit together and there just wasn't room for me to get to my bike, so I stood back and let everyone else get on with it. We weren't going anywhere in a hurry anyway, as there was an articulated lorry tight up against the bike area and the couple with their articulated tandem wouldn't be able to get out until that was gone. After 10 minutes or so, the lorries started their engines and gradually the ferry started emptying. As soon as the tandem had extricated itself, I jumped in and untied my bike, hooked up the panniers, etc. A quick wave from a crew member and I was away. I rode down the ferry ramp on to a spiral roadway and down to customs. My passport was scrutinized briefly and I was officially back in the United Kingdom.

I stopped to load my "Harwich to Amicii" route and I was away. I had 190 miles to ride; I had thought of doing it in one shot, as I have ridden that far in one day before, but on second thoughts it was better to split it in to two days, because if I rode it continuously I would arrive at the kennels at midnight or later, which would be a bit of an anticlimax as nobody would be there to meet me. In my current physical state I was even considering breaking it in to three days as at least I was sure I'd be able to manage that.

The weather was OK; I'd been pretty lucky up until now, only getting rain on a couple of days and even then it had cleared up pretty quickly. It was colder now though, 11 or 12 degrees, so I had my arm and leg warmers on and my warm gloves. There was a bit of a headwind too, not a roaring gale, but enough to slow me down. I rode out of Harwich on another EuroVelo route – the EV2 "Capitals Route", a route that links Dublin, London, Berlin, Warsaw, Minsk and Moscow. The route zig-zagged its way across Essex on B roads and back lanes, before meeting the river Colne at Wivenhoe, then followed the river upstream. On the opposite bank I could see the occasional pleasure boat that had broken free of its moorings and was somewhat the worse for wear, abandoned on the mud. The river Colne wound its way towards Colchester, but I left it and headed west before arriving at the centre. Just before I left the river, I passed the Colne light vessel, moored at the quayside and used as a training vessel by the Sea Cadets.

After a coupe of hours I passed through the village of Layer de la Haye and was tempted by the hoarding on the Layer Village Store, which offered the "Teacup Breakfast and Tea Room". I thought that it would probably be a good idea to try and eat something now, as I'd had nothing significant to eat for almost 48 hours. I walked in and towards the back of the shop, but it didn't look as if the tearoom was open. I confirmed this with the lady behind reception, who said that it just hadn't taken off. I bought some food from the shop and went and stood outside to eat.

The route I'd plotted wasn't too bad, considering I was in one of the most densely populated parts of the United Kingdom. A lot of the roads were quiet back lanes through agricultural land and mostly I was following EV2 and sometimes NCN 1. I don't remember doing this intentionally, but however it had happened it was working out OK. I stopped in Boreham at a supermarket to buy a 4 pack of sports drink and some chocolate. I think I was pretty much running on sugary drinks now, as there was precious little food inside me. I had hoped to find somewhere quiet and warm to sit and have something to eat and drink, but there's never a garden centre around when you really need one! I made a morning video and uploaded it to the group chat, because I think I'd been unintentionally maintaining radio silence since Rotterdam and people were beginning to ask about me. The lack of news was concerning some and although I did my best to keep the group chat updated I think I was in danger of being stopped and bundled in to an Amicii Rescue van at one stage. I wanted to finish under my own steam though – I'd come too far to give up now.

I rode on, passing through Chelmsford; which incidently has some excellent bike paths; before winding my way through the countryside towards Harlow. After 6 ½ hours on the road I stopped at a pub for lunch. I ordered a cheese baguette, but I struggled to eat it. It wasn't that I wasn't hungry, but as soon as I started to eat something I just felt full and couldn't force down any more. I ate half of my baguette and left. After Harlow I was directed down a path beside the river Stort, then up the river Lee navigation. This was very pretty and in an ideal world would make a fantastic cycle route, but unfortunately the path was bumpy, muddy and occasionally falling in to the canal. It almost makes a mockery of the National Cycle Network, especially after I'd ridden so many miles on exceptional cycle paths across Europe. I left the river Lee navigation at Hertford, then on the other side of the town I picked up on the Cole Green Way, which ran along a disused railway line to Welwyn Garden City. This again was a fantastic route, but would benefit from being surfaced, rather than a rough track.

I was running out of time now though. I had booked an Airbnb in Leighton Buzzard a few days ago, but with the extra day in Rotterdam I'd rescheduled it and now I messaged them again to say it looked like I might not make it. It was gone 6pm and it was still 20 miles away. I felt like I should be able to make it, but it would be gone 8pm if I did. I had lights, so it wasn't a case of getting there in daylight, it was just a case of getting there. I was just negotiating Welwyn when my phone rang. It was Jill. She wanted to know what I was going to do, she could see I still moving but didn't know what was planned. I explained the situation, but I don't think she was convinced. To set her mind at rest I said I'd abandon reaching Leighton Buzzard and see if I could find a hotel nearby. I looked for one on my app, but there wasn't one in the budget that I was prepared to pay. I carried on cycling.

After passing through Welwyn Garden City, I picked up the Ayot Greenway, which runs for three miles along a former branch line from Welwyn Garden City railway station towards Luton and Dunstable. I was just passing Harpendon when the phone ran again – i was Jill again. She wanted to know how my search for a hotel was going. I explained that there was nothing in Welwyn and that I was now passing Harpendon. She said "Harpendon's quite a big place, there must be somewhere in Harpendon!" Just at that moment a couple walked past, so I asked them. The reply wasn't encouraging, although the gentleman suggested a pub, which he knew had rooms. I thanked him and called the pub – they did indeed do accommodation, but they were fully booked. My last option was now Luton. It was on my route and there were several hotel chains there, I must be able to get somewhere to stay in Luton, surely?

It was another five miles on the greenway from Harpendon to Luton, but in all fairness it was an excellent cycle route – flat, surfaced, signposted, I take my hat off to Hertfordshire council. It still took me over half an hour to get there; by this stage my average speed had dropped from the giddy heights of 12 MPH down to something like 7 MPH and I didn't arrive until 7pm. The first hotel I came upon was the Premier Inn, but no, they didn't have a room. The lady there suggested the Hampton nearby. I called them from outside the Premier Inn. Yes, they did have a room – it was way more than I would have been willing to pay, but I took the room, I couldn't carry on any more. I rode the half mile or so to the hotel and pushed my bike in to the reception. Check-in undertaken, I stashed my bike in the left-luggage room and went to my room. It was 8pm and I was exhausted.

I don't remember much about the rest of the evening. I know I had a shower and I know I called Jill. I don't remember eating anything, which probably means I didn't…

*Wivenhoe, Colchester*

# DAY 18 – LUTON TO AMICII

90 miles

Another early start, but with luck it should be the final day, surely? I felt a lot better this morning and was determined to eat something other than chocolate, although that had at least got me here yesterday. I dressed and went downstairs to get some breakfast and managed some granola, followed by a small cooked breakfast. I wasn't impressed by the quality of the breakfast, so I didn't manage it all, but ate most of it. I went back to my room, changed in to my cycling clothes, applied a large dollop of German baby cream (bebe zartpflege) to my chamois and went downstairs to check out. I extricated my bike from the left-luggage room, hung on my bags and walked out in to the cold morning air.

The weather was similar to yesterday, grey, cloudy and about 10°C. The wind had dropped a little and had backed from the north-west to the south-west, so not quite as strong as yesterday and not on the nose. I loaded up my GPS route and set off towards Luton. Before long I was in Luton town centre, where I rode past the impressive town hall which, according to Historic England "was designed to create a powerful and highly visible landmark in the centre of the town. It was built in Neo-classical style, with Art Deco detailing in 1935-36". The rest of the town seemed pretty much on a par with modern towns anywhere, unsurprisingly as Luton suffered a large number of bombing raids in WW2 and damage to the town and its buildings was significant.

I was then directed to ride up the Luton-Dunstable busway, which I duly did for a short while before realising that I should be on the pavement, not the actual busway itself. The busway is a "guided busway", meaning that buses running on the busway are not steered by the driver, but rather by the kerbs on either side of the busway. The Luton busway is built on the route of a disused railway track, which makes me wonder if it would not just have been easier to reinstate the railway? All the same, I followed the busway for four or five miles before cutting through the centre of Dunstable and re-joining the same disused railway line (now no longer a busway) on the other side. This was originally the Dunstable branch line, which ran from Leighton Buzzard on the West Coast Main Line, to Welwyn Garden City on the East Coast Main Line, axed in the Beeching cuts in 1965. I rode the bike path for a couple of miles before it petered out and I was directed back on to the roads.

It took me an hour and a half to get to Leighton Buzzard this morning after a good night's rest. If I'd attempted that last night, it would have probably been more like two hours, meaning that I wouldn't have arrived at my Airbnb until about 9pm. In retrospect, it was probably a good call to stay in Luton last night, but I've always said that I have a PhD in hindsight.

I continued onwards in to Buckinghamshire on B roads, which were thankfully quite quiet, then with three hours and 25 miles under my belt I arrived in Winslow. I couldn't help but think of the Eagles song, 'Take it Easy", which features the line "Well, I'm a-standin' on a corner in Winslow, Arizona", so I may have sung a few chords, before I spotted a coffee shop and decided it was time for a break. I was obviously feeling a lot better by now, as I managed coffee, cake and a cookie, as well as my customary Coke.

Rested and warmed up a little, I continued through the countryside on NCN cycle routes, which were quiet lanes, if a little vague in direction. Outside Winslow, I rode past a railway, which I thought might have something to do with HS2, the UK's new high-speed railway from London to Birmingham. However, it turned out not to be HS2, but East West Rail, a planned new main railway line between East Anglia and South Wales. The section I saw was originally part of the Buckinghamshire railway, that ran between Bletchley to Banbury, abandoned in 1993. The proposed engineering works must have come as somewhat of a shock to the current owner of the stationmaster's house at Verney Junction.

An hour or so later, I passed through Buckingham, leaving the town on Stowe Avenue, a 1 ½ mile long, arrow-straight road leading to the Corinthian Arch belonging to Stowe House. Originally a manor house belonging to an abbey, the house has been successively developed over many centuries until it was rebuilt in 1683. It now houses the private Stowe school. My route then carried on through the lanes and B roads of Northamptonshire until I did cross the HS2 railway site north of Greatworth. I gather that in the long-term there will be a 1.5 mile long "Green Tunnel" at Greatworth, but at the moment it didn't look very green at all.

I hit the 50-mile mark at the village of Chacombe, near Banbury, which conveniently had an open pub, "The George and Dragon" and as it was about lunchtime I stopped for something to eat. I opted for the "soup of the day", as I thought that would go down easily, which it did. This was a good sign. I had 37 miles to go now, it looked very much like I was going to make it. My phone pinged and it was Ann, asking what time I thought I might arrive. I quickly did some maths and tentatively suggested 5pm.

The last stretch in to Banbury was along a bike path, then the Oxford canal walk. This worked out OK, but then I was directed down what was described as a "bike friendly path", but as the rough track got narrower and narrower I fell out with it and returned to the road. A quick manual recalculation and I passed Banbury to the north through a new housing estate. At least it had proper bike paths, albeit punctuated by roundabouts. I climbed out of Banbury towards Edgehill, which seemed to go on forever, not steep, but just continuously climbing. At the top of the hill, I joined the A422 Stratford Road, which I stayed on for the next 12 miles. Although it was an A road, it was reasonably quiet, I guess the majority of the traffic was on the M40. I was rewarded by a long downhill stretch almost immediately, down "Sun Rising Hill", I couldn't throw caution to the winds though as there were a couple of bends in it. I still reached 33 MPH though! The A422 undulated uphill and down past fields and through villages, all the time getting closer and closer to Stratford-upon-Avon. It was almost as if I saw Stratford as the final destination, which of course it wasn't, but I knew once I got there, it wasn't far.

Apart from having to shelter under a tree from a passing shower, I progressed steadily, finally turning off of the A422 to bypass Stratford to the south. I then joined the Stratford greenway, which runs on the route of a disused railway. I stopped briefly for a final cup of coffee and piece of cake. I only had 15 miles to go, so I thought I'd indulge myself. I continued a couple of miles on the greenway, then my GPS beeped at me, saying I should take a right turn. I obviously hadn't paid much attention to this section of the route, as the next couple of miles were on those "bike friendly paths" again, although I'd have described it more as "riding through a field of onions on a bumpy track". I then rode down the bank of the river Avon on a similar track, before eventually appearing in the village of Welford-on-Avon.

In Welford, there was a "road closed" sign and I began to think that the Gods were conspiring against me to prevent me from reaching my goal! I asked a gentleman walking his dog if the road was really closed and he said I could probably get through on my bike. That was good news, as the alternative would have involved a lengthy detour.

On and on I rode, getting closer and closer to my destination. These were roads I knew well, having ridden them a number of times. Before long I was in Wixford, then Dunnington, Radford, past "The Wheelbarrow Castle" pub, one final uphill… Where's the turning? There it is! I had arrived. It was 5.07pm.

As I rolled down the track towards the kennels, I could hear the cheers of the reception committee who, despite the fact I must have been pretty smelly after 10 hours in the saddle, greeted me with hugs and happy faces and more importantly, tea!

*Tired, dirty, smelly, but happy*

# CHAPTER 14. EPILOGUE

After my celebratory cup of tea I grabbed a lift home with Tracey – I did consider riding, but that thought was soon drummed out of my head! It wasn't long before we arrived and Jill let me in. Stella was shut in another room, so I went and slowly opened the door. Out she bounded, straight past me! Only when she turned around did it register that I was even there, but what a reception I received when she did! I think it's safe to say she had missed me, but possibly not as much as I had missed her. In the last 18 days I'd had some highs and lows. I thought that I'd hit a low spot on the road from Szeged to Budapest when dicing with articulated lorries, but that was nothing compared to contracting what was probably norovirus in Rotterdam. The high spot was today, being greeted by Stella. What drove me on was the thought of getting home to Stella (and Jill!), plus the knowledge that every penny raised would help other dogs like Stella find their forever home.

In the end, we raised nearly £7,500 for Amicii, far, far more than I'd ever dreamt of. I rode 1700.79 miles in total, an average of 94.48 miles/day.

# ACKNOWLEDGEMENTS

Behind every adventure is a team of people who help to make it possible, this one is no different. First and foremost, I have to start by thanking my wife, Jill. Without her support and patience, none of this would ever have been possible. She held the fort and looked after the dogs while I was away gallivanting across Europe.

I also have to extend my gratitude to all those in Amicii Dog Rescue UK who humoured me and my foolish ideas and provided me with much-needed moral support along the way: Ann Davies, Jan Williams, Tracey Baker and not least "Captain" Ann Pursey. Thanks also go out to Kelly Magee at Immingham Dogs Home, for her support in "challenge one".

To the team of Amicii Dog Romania: Dora, Daniela, Ioana and Bianca, who welcomed me with open arms at the rescue, all of whom give up their own valuable free time as well as managing their own jobs. Visiting the shelter brought the true purpose of this journey to the fore.

Finally, special thanks to Cristina, who rescued Stella from the roadside and nursed her back to health. Without her care, I'd never of had the privilege of offering Stella a home.

## About The Author

Steve Cuthbertson is an eternal dreamer trapped inside the body of a middle-aged man. He dreams of travelling the world by bicycle but has to settle for a job in IT instead. He has lived and worked in South America and Antarctica and was awarded the Polar Medal by HRH Prince (now King) Charles in Buckingham Palace. When he's not cycling or fixing computers he likes to walk with his dog, Stella.

Find out more at blog.goingtothedogs.co.uk

## OTHER BOOKS BY STEVEN

This is Steven's first book, although he has started at least two others. You never know, if this one goes down well, he might just finish them!

## Can I Ask A Favour?

If you enjoyed this book, found it useful or otherwise then I'd really appreciate it if you would post a short review on Amazon. I do read all the reviews personally so that I can write what people want to read.

Printed in Great Britain
by Amazon